ALWAYS

BEEN

LOVED

ADVANCE PRAISE FOR
ALWAYS BEEN LOVED

"God's love is something that we can so easily misunderstand or misrepresent, and I feel the truth of the gospel pulsing through the pages of *Always Been Loved* from beginning to end. I found myself truly encouraged by the beautiful truth of the book's message. It made me think about God's love in some ways I never had before."

—Hannah Reynolds,
Published Author, Featured in *South Carolina's Emerging Writers: An Anthology of Fiction* and *The Mountain Laurel*

Discovering God's
True Feelings for You

ALWAYS
BEEN
LOVED

Celeste Hawkins

AMBASSADOR INTERNATIONAL
GREENVILLE, SOUTH CAROLINA & BELFAST, NORTHERN IRELAND
www.ambassador-international.com

Always Been Loved

Discovering God's True Feelings for You
©2022 by Celeste Hawkins
All rights reserved.

ISBN: 978-1-64960-034-9
eISBN: 978-1-64960-035-6

Cover Design by Celeste Hawkins
Interior Typesetting by Hannah Nichols and Dentelle Design

Unless otherwise indicated, all Scripture quotations are taken from the Holy Bible, New Living Translation, copyright © 1996, 2004, 2015 by Tyndale House Foundation. Used by permission of Tyndale House Publishers, Inc., Carol Stream, Illinois 60188. All rights reserved.

Scripture quotations marked (ERV) are taken from the HOLY BIBLE: EASY-TO-READ VERSION © 2014 by Bible League International. Used by permission. All rights reserved.

AMBASSADOR INTERNATIONAL
Emerald House
411 University Ridge, Suite B14
Greenville, SC 29601
United States
www.ambassador-international.com

AMBASSADOR BOOKS
The Mount
2 Woodstock Link
Belfast, BT6 8DD
Northern Ireland, United Kingdom
www.ambassadormedia.co.uk

The colophon is a trademark of Ambassador, a Christian publishing company.

CONTENTS

ACKNOWLEDGMENTS

I offer my sincerest thanks to the following people who have helped me on this journey to publish my first book:

Lucas, thank you for believing in me on the days when I don't. You are truthfully the best husband in the world, as far as I'm concerned. Because of your kind actions and your words of grace and your quick forgiveness over the years, I've really begun to believe that God does love me. You constantly remind me of His love for me! And I hope I can show others His love the way you've shown it to me.

Mom, thank you for reading all those bedtime stories. Your love for books—and your love for the Lord—they've never left me.

Kerrie, thank you for reading this book and sharing your thoughts with me. Thank you for being both a wonderful sister and friend. I remember Friday night visits to Barnes and Noble with you and Mom, as well as all those stories we started to write together as kids (which all had mostly the same plotline). That's really where writing began for me.

Jimmy, Justin, Tiffany, Caitlin, Payton, and Jamison, thank you for believing in me and supporting me as a writer over the years—even when it meant putting on those Christmas plays before presents!

Calvary Chapel church family, thank you for your faithful prayers, encouragement, and love. I often find myself telling other people that everyone should have a church family like you! And I mean that from the bottom of my heart.

Hannah Reynolds, you have probably read more of my first drafts of stories, poems, and books than anyone else. Thank you for always taking the time to do that and to encourage me to keep writing, dear friend.

Leah Hill, thank you for not accepting any of my excuses and for forcing me to go to Write2Ignite, where I started to actually believe I could be an author. If you hadn't, I might not have ever met Dr. Samuel Lowry or ended up publishing this book. I owe you big time!

Dr. Samuel Lowry and the Ambassador International team, thank you for believing in this book from day one and helping me along every step of the way to get to the point of sharing it with the world. You are incredible!

Daniel Blackaby, thank you for the simple advice to write consistently every day. Because I listened to you, I finally finished my first book! Thank you, too, for your in-depth review of and much-needed advice about this book. It's better because of you.

My English teachers over the years—Andrea Armstrong, Dr. Greg Bruce, Rick Clinard, Dr. Cheryl Collier, Sandy Crumpler, Dr. Deborah DeCiantis, Dr. Julia Drummond, Lucy Malenke, Mark Perry, Valerie Reed, Dr. Cathy Sepko, Dr. Hiewon Shin, Michelle Hall Snider, and Dr. Becky Thompson—thank you for sharing your love for the written word with me and for inspiring me to write!

My North Greenville University family, thank you for always cheering me on! You have an irreplaceable spot in my heart.

My Lord and Savior, thank You for loving me from eternity. All my words are for You.

PREFACE

This is a book about God and you and the way He's been hopelessly in love with you forever.

It's mad.

It's nonsensical.

It's unbelievable.

And yet it's true.

You probably haven't given this that much thought. Maybe, like me, you grew up singing "Jesus Loves Me" in children's church, but, when you graduated up to "big service" with the adults, it felt like every message became about what you needed to do to live right or, more likely, what you needed to stop doing if you wanted to stay in good standing with God.

Like don't cuss when you stump your toe.

And don't go to bars.

And don't forget to have your devotions as soon as you wake up and right before you go to bed at night.

Somewhere along the way of living with God, you started to believe that you were working for His approval, and the only way He could possibly be happy with you at the end of the day is if you made sure your good outweighed the bad things you'd done.

You began to feel like He's more of a master, a boss, or even a slave driver.

In theory, you lived like you were forgiven. But in reality, you lived like you had to keep all the rules.

And you still think the constant nagging at the back of your heart—that you haven't done enough, haven't helped enough, aren't enough—is from Him.

I know because this was me a year ago. This is still me on my worst days. But what began to change it all for me was this one word that found me just after one of the worst years of my life:

"I pray that your life will be strong in love and be built on love. And I pray that you and all God's holy people will have the power to understand the greatness of Christ's love—how wide, how long, how high, and how deep that love is. Christ's love is greater than anyone can ever know, but I pray that you will be able to know that love. Then you can be filled with everything God has for you" (Eph. 3:17b-19 Easy-to-Read Version).

For the first time, it hit me: my life is only as full as how much I understand God's love for me. And I'd been living my whole life very close to empty, measuring its greatness by my goodness. Honestly, I'd never taken five minutes to think about what it meant that God loved me, even though I could quote verses about it and tell you the story of the cross.

Over the past year, I've made it my mission to find out what it means that God loves me. What has He done to show me that? How can I see His love? And how does that change my life?

The Lord has been breaking into my heart with His love as I've dived deeper into it, and I've begun to realize that this love—this unbelievable love—is really the only reason we can come to Him in the first place. But it's also the only way we can stay with Him, too.

God's love is what fills us, what compels us, and what makes us become and do all God plans for us. And without God's love in the picture, we're just empty, broken, and powerless people willing ourselves to live a little nicer than our neighbors down the street.

Without a right view of God's undying love for us, we're bound to misunderstand the past, His plans, and even our own purpose.

So my hope is that this book can be for you what it's been for me as I've written it: it can be like a summer vacation—for your soul; comfort food on a Sunday afternoon—for your soul; or a cold shower after working in the heat for hours—for your soul.

I'm hoping that for a few brief moments in this short life, we can step away together from the have-to-dos of our faith into the have-to-knows. So, while I believe strongly in the change that Jesus Christ makes in every life that lets Him into it, this book is an ask-free zone, a try-free zone, a do-free zone.

I hope together we can just take a step back, point our eyes upward, and scale the immensity of God's love for us, a love that's eternal, unfailing, and faithful.

Then, we'll discover a greater fullness in our lives than ever before! Because love casts out fear. Love transforms hearts. Love completes us.

See, this isn't about being a better person or making God happier with you. This book is about uncovering the once-in-a-lifetime, out-of-this-world, you've-never-known-anything-else-like-it love that God feels for you every moment and becoming whole because of that.

And this book is a brief look—really only a scratch on the surface—at what God has done, what God does, and what God will do to show you this unchangeable truth: you're loved.

You've always been loved.

AUTHOR'S NOTE

Dear Reader,

The story of God's love—such an intimate and personal love—merits an intimate and personal telling.

That's why I've chosen to relay all these great truths about God's love for us as if they were written by Him, coming right from His own lips (instead of mine) and into your heart. Hopefully, this allows you to experience His message for you the same way I did so many times during the writing process, and you'll feel like He's speaking directly to you. Yes, you!

I hope the result will be that your heart is encouraged, amazed, and filled by the unfailing love of our generous and merciful God.

In Him,

Celeste

CHAPTER 1

LOVE IS NOT (JUST) WHAT GOD DOES

God is love.

—*1 John 4:8b*

Dear Loved One,

You might think of love as just one of the many things that I do. But it's so much more than that: it is who I am at the very core.

Because what you do comes from who you are. Your actions, they are only a reflection of your identity. You can never *do* outside unless you first *are* inside (Matt. 12:35).

That is why I am able to love so fully, so freely, so faithfully in the way that I will show you now, because I am love. And love is Me.

It isn't just that it is in Me. Or that I have it. Or that I do it.

I am love. Love itself. The definition of love, the substance of love, the epitome of love.

This is important for you to see and know. Otherwise, you might think of love as separate from Me, as part of the creation I invented many years ago.

In a sense it is true: I am the very creator of love, the very inventor of it, the very initiator of it. But in another sense, love was never created, invented, or initiated. It always was.

Since it is who I am, it has been around for as long as Me. There was never a moment in the history of time, or before that, that love wasn't already existing. Because there was never a moment when I was not already existing.

When you read "In the beginning God" (Gen. 1:1), you can see love, too. Because I am God, and I am love. It was right there with Me.

To separate love from your view of Me—to take it out of the equation for even a moment of My existence—is to make Me un-whole: it is to dismember Me, distort Me, misunderstand Me.

I am love as much as I am God. And I cannot stop loving any more than I can stop being God (Ps. 102:25-27).

It may be strange to think about: that I have always been love, and I have always loved.

Even before My speech turned from sound to sand, from breath to birds, from words to worlds, and all came into existence, I loved even back then. When there was no one else to love yet, I was still love. And I still loved. I loved Myself—Father, Son, and Spirit of Me—even when there was no one else existing (John 17:24-26).

This love—when Love loved Love before the world was ever created—this was the earliest love, and it was My love. And if that was all there had been, I would still have been happy in My love. Because I am not a needy God. I have no needs. I am sufficient and satisfied simply in being Me (Acts 17:24-25).

I love, but before even that, I am love. Love itself. And perfect love is always full and whole.

The story could have ended here, but it doesn't. No, it only begins here: with Me, with Love.

Love,

God

DEEPER STUDY

- Read 1 John 4:7-21.

POINT TO PONDER

- How does seeing love as who God is—instead of only what He does—change how you view Him? _____

_____

_____

_____

_____

_____

_____

_____

_____

_____

_____

_____

_____

_____

_____

_____

_____

_____

_____

_____

_____

_____

_____

_____

_____

_____

CHAPTER 2

GOD LOVES YOU AS MUCH AS HE LOVES HIMSELF

'I am in them and you are in me.
May they experience such perfect unity that the world will know
that you sent me and that you love them as much as you love me.
Father, I want these whom you have given me to be with me where I am.
Then they can see all the glory you gave me
because you loved me even before the world began!'
—*John 17:23-24*

Dear Loved One,

I have to tell you more about My love, a part of it that I think you will probably never begin to understand: I love you like I love Myself.

Remember when I told you that I have always been love and always loved? When no one else existed but Me, I loved Myself with all My heart. And I was so happy in that love.

But even then, I knew My plans to create you. And even though you didn't know Me, I knew you. And I loved you with all My heart (Eph. 1:4).

I loved Myself before the world began. And I loved you as much as I loved Myself: Father, Son, and Spirit. So I loved you before the world was created and before you had a heartbeat or ever took a breath.

Because to love someone as much as you love someone else you've loved since eternity, you would also have to love that person since as long ago as eternity.

Yes, to love you as much as I love Myself, when I have loved Myself since eternity, would mean I have also loved you since eternity.

An eternity-long love could never be comparable to another love, except another eternity-long love.

And that is what I have for you: an eternity-long love.

You can see it now—can't you—in My words to you? The most important commands I've ever given anyone were to love Me with their heart, soul, and mind and to love others as they love themselves (Matt. 22:34-40). I am in these commands. This is a God-sized love.

Loving with My whole self, that is what I do. I am full of love in every fiber of My being (Joel 2:13). There's no part of Me where love is absent.

Loving as I love Myself, that is what I do. Just as wholly as I love Myself, I love you, too.

I never ask you to be something I am not. When I ask you to love others as you love yourself, I am calling you to join in being who I am, in loving as I love.

And I love others, and I love you, as I love My very Self.

Love,

God

DEEPER STUDY

- Read John 17:20-26.

POINT TO PONDER

- What are some ways you can think of that God has shown you He loves you as much as He loves Himself? _____

_____

CHAPTER 3

WHAT HAPPENED BEFORE THE BEGINNING

Even before he made the world, God loved us . . .
—Ephesians 1:4a

Dear Loved One,

Yes, it's true that I love you as I love Myself. But how could it be that I've loved you forever?

I have existed forever and loved Myself for as long, so that may make more sense to you. But how could I love you forever when you weren't even born yet?

Do you want to imagine loving someone deeply and personally that you've never met before—much less someone who doesn't even exist yet? Well, maybe you can begin to understand that impossibility when you think of your future children (I John 3:1). That is how I loved you back before I made the world.

Picture your baby cradled in your arms, that newborn face looking up at you. Maybe she'll have big, brown eyes and beautiful, long eyelashes like you. Maybe he'll have soft, curly blond hair like your spouse did in the pictures from childhood.

You know, maybe he'll love to write and read like you do, or she'll be able to fix computers in just a moment like your spouse. But whether or not you share any of these similarities, the child will be yours. And somewhere in your heart, whether now or during the months of your pregnancy, you'll find you can love her already just for that simple fact.

You will love him already.

In the same way that expecting parents prepare the nursery before their child is born—decorating and putting up the curtains and building the crib—there will already be a room in your heart with her name on it; there will already be a place in your heart waiting for him.

And at this moment, as you picture, only imagine, this joy, you finally know how it was for Me all those years ago before you or anyone else came into existence, when My plan for creation hadn't come to life yet.

I loved you.

See, in some mysterious way, the most permanent thing about you, about every person who has walked this earth I made, isn't even your own existence; that has only started really quite recently in the timeline of history.

And like a short breath huffed into cold morning air, your lives are only a moment, and then they will disappear, vanish (Ps. 144:3-4; James 4:14).

But before you were born, I loved you. The most permanent, longest lasting thing about you, here long before you were born, is the eternal love I've always had for you. I set My sights on you when you were still yet to come (Ps. 139:15).

I loved you before the beginning of yourself; I loved you before the beginning of anything.

And I love you now with that same forever love.

Love,

God

DEEPER STUDY

- Read Psalm 139.

POINT TO PONDER

- If God chose to love you before you were born—and able to do good things or bad things—then what do you think was the basis of His decision to love you?

_____

_____

_____

_____

_____

_____

_____

_____

_____

_____

_____

_____

_____

_____

_____

_____

_____

_____

_____

_____

_____

_____

_____

_____

CHAPTER 4

WHAT GOD DOES FOR FUN

Where is another God like you,
who pardons the guilt of the remnant,
overlooking the sins of his special people?
You will not stay angry with your people forever,
because you delight in showing unfailing love.

—*Micah 7:18*

Dear Loved One,

Have you ever stopped to wonder what I do for enjoyment, only because I want to and not because I have to? Love is one of those things.

Really, everything that I do is just because I want to, in My goodness. I do not love because I am obligated to, but because I want to. I have no obligations to anyone else. No one has ever given anything to Me that I didn't give them first (I Cor. 4:7); I owe no one anything.

Remember, one of My names speaks of this: "'I Am Who I Am'" (Exod. 3:14 ERV). I will be who I will be—not because any external force puts that pressure on Me but because that is what I choose to be.

Everything that I am, everything that I do, everything that I say is because I choose to be that, do that, say that. My nature directs every decision I make, but that doesn't mean I am just a machine. Many times, I make a decision because I find enjoyment in that decision.

Of course, My enjoyment is important to Me; I lent you My emotions and capacity for happiness when I created you to be like Me (Gen. 1:27).

I delight.

I enjoy.

I laugh.

I smile.

I sing for joy.

I've given you glimpses of what makes Me really excited and giddy. You can see what I do because I want to and because I delight in doing it. And it is this: to love unworthy people. To show mercy. To bring people toward Me (2 Pet. 3:9).

I love you, I love anyone, because I choose to. More than that, I choose to love because in making that decision to love I find great enjoyment. I know loving is the very best way to live; that is why I gave you the command to love as the most important of all (Col. 3:14). I desire for you to know this greatest of joys: to love!

I love because I want to do that (Rom. 11:32), and it makes Me happy, and I find enjoyment in it—just the day-to-day loving of people who love Me imperfectly back. People like you.

No one has ever asked Me to love them, and no one can make Me love them more. I already love you because I enjoy it and because I want to and because I find pleasure in it.

I find such pleasure in loving you! Showing you love and undeserved mercy is one of the greatest, most enjoyable, most pleasurable pastimes for Me, the Creator of all the earth—who has made all things (1 Cor. 8:6; Rev. 4:11), who holds all things together (Col. 1:17), and who owns all things (1 Cor. 3:21-23).

What do you give to someone who already has everything? For Me, what I wanted when I could choose to do anything in all the world was the opportunity to love more. For the God who has everything, I still just enjoy putting My love on others and delighting in them and allowing them to share in My love.

I have no greater delight than to put My mercy on someone and draw them close to Me. I give My heart so freely—though the love returned is always unequal to Mine (1 John 4:10)—because it brings Me enjoyment.

Yes, I am a peculiar God who finds enjoyment in loving you, who loves you for the fun of it, and who loves you just because I want to.

Love,

God

DEEPER STUDY

- Read Exodus 33:12-23.

POINT TO PONDER

- God delights in showing mercy to undeserving people. How do you imagine the world would be different if He didn't?_____

_____

_____

_____

_____

_____

_____

_____

_____

_____

_____

_____

_____

_____

_____

_____

_____

CHAPTER 5

WHERE ALL LOVE COMES FROM

Love comes from God. Everyone who loves has become God's child.
And so everyone who loves knows God.
Anyone who does not love does not know God,
because God is love.

—*1 John 4:7b-8 (ERV)*

Dear Loved One,

I never *needed* anyone else to love besides Myself. But love tends to want to love more. And I wanted to love more.

So I decided to create the world with people to love.

Because I have love to give and to spare and to share, and still there is more in Me. Love pours out of Me. It is a well that never goes dry, even when more love comes up from it.

I am love, but also all real love comes from Me (1 John 4:7). No love can exist apart from coming straight from My heart. There is no love that comes from another source or another place.

Today, when you love another person, that love is only a fulfillment of My love (1 John 4:12) and not an origination of your own love from your own heart. Because My love is like matter: it cannot be created or destroyed. It can only change hands.

When you borrow love from Me to give it to others, you'll find it becomes imperfect in your grimy hands—all stained and smeared up and blemished. You will never be able to give perfect love to them, though I have given perfect love to you.

Your heart is not pure like Mine. Your hands are not clean like Mine. So your love is not perfect like Mine.

You know you love others sometimes; there are brilliant moments when you see the flecks of love, reflecting from Me onto you with an unearthly selflessness.

But then, to those same ones you love, sometimes you speak harsh, angry words in spite.

You pull away when the love is too hard to give.

You keep the record book called *All the Times They Hurt Me*.

That book may be long. Others have hurt you deeply, and yet they said they loved you, too.

Don't be confused, dear one. Hearts are capable both of love and of hate. Remember, though, what true love looks like: it does no wrong at all to another (Rom. 13:10). It never treats the one it loves wrongly. It does not take life; it gives up its life (1 John 3:16). So, it is always life-giving.

My love is like that. My love is a perfect love that always treats you rightly. My love is the real thing. I can love perfectly because I am perfect love.

No, I am not the only one who loves now. But I am certainly still the best at loving. Remember: love is who I am (I John 4:8). My love defines the very nature of who I am. And without My love, no one else could love, even with their imperfect, inconsistent love.

When you are hurting because you have been loved imperfectly by others, you can always return to Me. I will still love you perfectly. And you can still look for the good in that lesser love. Because all love comes from Me, even the imperfect ones. They've simply been handed off by imperfect love-sharers. Oh, I hope you can sense My love even there.

But I hope, more than that, that you will always come back to Me, the original source of love. My love is the original love, the first love, and the best love. All love comes from Me, and I will always be willing to give you as much love as you need and more.

Love,

God

DEEPER STUDY

- Read 1 Corinthians 13.

POINT TO PONDER

- Even despite the imperfect ways that others have loved you, how can you see remnants of the perfect love of God in their love?_____

_____

_____

_____

_____

_____

_____

_____

_____

_____

_____

_____

_____

_____

_____

_____

_____

_____

_____

CHAPTER 6

THE UNFAIRNESS OF LOVE

Even before he made the world, God loved us and chose us in Christ
to be holy and without fault in his eyes.
God decided in advance to adopt us into his own family
by bringing us to himself through Jesus Christ.
This is what he wanted to do, and it gave him great pleasure.
So we praise God for the glorious grace he has poured out on us
who belong to his dear Son.

—Ephesians 1:4-6

Dear Loved One,

Part of the great wonder, the great mystery of love, is the choosing. And I chose to love you before I made the world and before you were born.

Before I tell you why, let Me ask you something: Why didn't you choose to marry someone else? Why didn't you choose someone else to be your best friend? When you could've chosen anyone in the whole world, why did you pick the one you picked?

Others were prettier, nicer, taller. Yes, some had more money, more talent, more education.

But still, you picked the one you picked. That's what love is: a choice.

I have made a choice, too. I have chosen to love every person I have ever created, even the murderers and the adulterers, the liars and the thieves. The worst offenders on My list, I still love even them. Without discrimination, I love every person in the world (John 3:16).

And I don't want a single soul to die without turning towards Me and My love for them (2 Pet. 3:9). Not even one! That is how great My love is.

Another choice I've made is to adopt children into My loving family. I know this can seem unfair at first glance: Why do only some "get in" to My family? This is a great mystery to you.

But hear Me: every person who accepts My invitation has a place in My home and at My table (John 1:12; 2 Cor. 5:20)! Whoever you are, you are welcome here.

Yes, My love is global, for everyone. But it is also deeply personal, meant for your individual heart.

For before I ever made the world, I knew all that would happen. And before a moment of time had passed, I had a plan to bring everything together to Me (Eph. 1:10). See, as the same One who could see the story of redemption, I could also see the story of the fall and brokenness in this world, not only across the world but in every person's heart.

I could see you and your mistakes and sins and the times you would forget Me, deny Me, and fall away. I could see your hurts and weaknesses and terrible, nasty habits. I could see the evil in your heart and the parts of you that still don't want Me yet, even today.

And still, I chose to love you!

I didn't choose you for anything that you were or could do. At that time, you were no one and had done nothing (2 Tim. 1:9). But I could see everything that your life would be, and I still chose you regardless. I chose you, and you can't even begin to understand why. It makes no logical sense because you were broken beyond repair, unless I stepped in.

And I hope that somehow, you will think of how I choose unworthy people like you to be loved and it will make your heart explode with wonder and thankfulness.

I know sometimes that is not your reaction at all. You might feel like it's unfair that some receive My mercy and others never do (Rom. 9:18).

In this "fair world" you wish for, I have to tell you this: I wouldn't have shown mercy to anyone. I would have picked none of you to be recipients of My goodness. For mercy, by definition, is not deserved. So, it wouldn't exist if everyone had what was "fair" coming to them.

If I gave each person what they deserved in all fairness, they would have been separated from Me forever, because that's how serious sin and rebellion are to Me.

But it's not because of anything that you have done or anything that you are that I chose you (Rom. 9:16). Really, I picked the most unlikely ones. Many I chose were the humble ones, the broken ones, the poor ones, the unwise ones (1 Cor. 1:26). I picked those who were nothing and had nothing.

Oh, I picked you because I delight and find joy in showing mercy to people who don't deserve it!

If I were only fair, I would've picked no one to be Mine. But because I am merciful, I chose children for My family, and it would seem at random, not based on anything you had done. Remember: if I were to base it on what you had done, I wouldn't have picked you.

I could see exactly what you were, and I could foresee the times of happiness and times of hurt, times of victory and times of struggle, times of plenty and times of need. But love chooses to love during all those kinds of times. And that's what I chose.

I looked to all the times ahead and decided to be joined to My family. I call you My children, and I call you My wife. I'm married to My Church, made up of a bride that I picked and chose and committed to love even on her worst days. I would showcase My love by bringing glory to My name through her, made up of people who are unworthy but loved.

And I don't stop loving you. Love is always choosing. You choose a spouse, and with that choice, you have forsaken and given up your rights to choose any other person to love in that way. So you choose them again day after day.

So have I done—not out of hatred or out of evil or out of unfairness—but out of love: I have chosen and picked and singled out My people to be the love of My life (Rom. 8:33).

And that love for you does not depend on your performance or your actions or your abilities or your goodness. My love for you depends only on My love for you! And it cannot change, and it has not stopped since before time began ticking and the world began turning and you began existing in this world.

My love is a love that chooses, for reasons unknown to you but known to Me. And you will come to see it's a love that's not fair—but in the best of ways.

Because it's a love that is merciful and unearned and undeserved.

Love,

God

DEEPER STUDY

- Read Romans 9:1-16 and Romans 11:25-36.

POINT TO PONDER

- This chapter touches on a very sensitive topic, even for Christians. How do you make sense of God's love for all people and His love for those He adopts into His family?_____

_____

_____

_____

_____

_____

_____

CHAPTER 7

THE BIG REVEAL

For the law was given through Moses, but God's unfailing love and faithfulness came through Jesus Christ. No one has ever seen God. But the unique One, who is himself God, is near to the Father's heart. He has revealed God to us.
—John 1:17-18

Dear Loved One,

Love like Mine can't sit back forever and watch. Love must show itself; it must take action (1 John 3:18).

There was a time before I showed My full love, though. So, when you read My Storybook, it may seem I only started to love the world halfway through it. In reality, I always loved with My whole heart. I was just waiting for the right moment to show that love, a Big Reveal.

All the years when the world kept worsening and worsening, you turned away from Me more and more. It all began just days into creation; our beautiful relationship was broken.

And the curse of sin cut quick: one day you were eating forbidden fruit (Gen. 3:6), and the next you were killing your own brother (Gen. 4:8).

So I gave you more rules and laws. They helped you figure out how to live, but they didn't actually help you to live that way; their intention was never to make you right with Me, but to show you that you weren't right with Me and couldn't be right with Me on your own (Rom. 3:19-20). You would need My help; you would need Me to save you from all this. This was all part of the plan.

I was preparing you for the Big Reveal. I loved you even then. I loved you "so much" (John 3:16 ERV) even then.

See, I knew it would take more than guidelines and checklists to bring you back to My heart. First, I would have to show you My heart and reveal My love to you in big lights. And I wouldn't use the impersonal law to do that.

And that love would break into your heart and transform it, make it a home that could finally receive My love and love Me in return. Because the Big Reveal was to send Myself, to show you love with skin on it.

Through Moses on the mountain, I revealed My holiness by offering laws. Those are written in the Old Testament.

But through My Son Jesus on the hill, I revealed My unfailing love by offering salvation. I sent Jesus to finally reveal Myself to you in full, so you could finally know that love I so loved you with.

This was what I decided to do: to reveal My love to you. And Jesus was the perfect one to reveal it. You'll see.

Love,

God

DEEPER STUDY

- Read Titus 3:3-7.

POINT TO PONDER

- How did the coming of Jesus change how we saw God from that point forward?_____

_____

_____

_____

_____

_____

_____

_____

CHAPTER 8

THE HARDEST MOMENT FOR GOD TO LOVE YOU

Yes, God loved the world so much that he gave his only Son,
so that everyone who believes in him would not be lost but have eternal life.
God sent his Son into the world. He did not send him to judge the world guilty,
but to save the world through him.

—John 3:16-17 (ERV)

Dear Loved One,

I love you with a love that drove Me to give up what is dearest to Me: Jesus, My Son. It was the hardest thing I ever had to do, and yet it was the only way I could reveal the kind of love I have for you.

In the same way I loved you before I made the world, I loved My own Son. He was part of Me, and He had never rejected Me or turned away from My love. He was flawless. He had always done My will.

And still, He said "yes" to My will when it meant that He had to be born into this broken creation and rejected by everyone around Him and eventually crushed by Me. When I sent Him, I already knew what would happen: He would die as I personally took every sin committed by every person from every moment in time and laid it on Him in all its heaviness, so that He, the Innocent One, would die for those sins Himself (Isa. 53:6).

My heart was so divided. Can you begin to imagine the pain of losing your own son? Of course, it made Me happy to send Him because it meant people could experience My salvation. But it also hurt My heart to let Him leave My presence.

I showed the extent of My love by giving up a gift that was one of a kind; this wasn't one son of many. I gave My one and only Son.

I loved you so much that I was willing to give away My most valuable, dearest, and beloved Son, to send Him from heaven's gates and enter this world. I risked it all and gave it all to give every person—every single person—the opportunity and the chance and the invitation to be right with Me and live with Me forever.

Sending Jesus wasn't Plan B when I noticed you couldn't keep My Word anymore. My plan was always to send Jesus Christ, so He could bring everything back to its rightful place with Me (Eph. 1:10). I knew the cost of this plan from the very beginning. I was willing to see it through even back then.

I was willing to give up My life so you could live with Me forever.

My love has already given the most difficult thing to give: My Son. And it still gives Him freely. Now you must know: if I would give Him up for you, even My very own Son, then there is certainly nothing else I would possibly hold back from you (Rom. 8:32).

Love,

God

DEEPER STUDY

- Read Ephesians 1:3-14.

POINT TO PONDER

- When God gave Jesus to us to show us His love, what else came along with this one gift of His Son?_____

_____

_____

_____

_____

_____

CHAPTER 9

EVERY LITTLE THING JESUS DID

"I have loved you even as the Father has loved me. Remain in my love.
When you obey my commandments, you remain in my love,
just as I obey my Father's commandments and remain in his love.
I have told you these things so that you will be filled with my joy.
Yes, your joy will overflow! This is my commandment:
Love each other in the same way I have loved you.
There is no greater love than to lay down one's life for one's friends."
—*John 15:9-13*

Dear Loved One,

Yes, I gave up My Son Jesus for you to reveal My love to you. And Jesus was the full explanation of My love for you during every moment of His life on earth.

When He healed the sick, that was a picture of My love.

When He fed the hungry, that was a picture of My love.

When He taught the crowds about My kingdom, that was a picture of My love.

When He granted forgiveness to the adulteress, that was My love.

When He opened blind eyes, that was My love.

When He invited tax collectors to be His disciples, that was My love.

Every action, every word, every little gesture of Jesus was Me and My love. It would have been one thing for Me to tell you I loved you, but another altogether to show you My love. And that's what I did through Jesus. You can see My love on full display—in Him, if you will look closely (Rom. 8:39).

If you have seen Jesus, you have seen Me (John 14:9). If you have seen Jesus, you have seen My kindness. If you have seen Jesus, you have seen My love, My dear.

Then at the end of His life as a man, He died. And even in His death, He showed you My love. When He willingly died for every person on the cross, even you, that was a picture of My love. Oh, don't miss it! That was the very climax of Our love story.

When He took the thorny crown on His head, that was My love.

When He took the nails in His hands, that was My love.

When His blood dripped down from the wooden cross onto the ground, that was My love.

There is no greater love than that! Real love always leads to a cross, dying to self so that others can have life (I John 3:16). That is what My love did for you in Jesus. Even in His final moments, He was still demonstrating My love to you.

Oh, I know you have had an imperfect life. There have been pains and heartbreaks and struggles. You have probably forgotten sometimes that I love you. You may have even become tired of hearing of Jesus. You want to hear that I love you, but you don't want to hear about Him.

I can't do that. I have to talk about Jesus when I talk about loving you. If you want to know how I really love you, look at Him. If you want to know how to love others, look at Him.

Because consider this: what more can someone do to show you their love than die for you? It's impossible to do more than that. In that one gift, you are giving everything. And that is what I did when I died on the cross for you: I gave up everything for you (2 Cor. 8:9).

Through Jesus, I lived every moment of My life on earth showing you My love in person, and then I died for you in a final grand gesture—so you might see the love I have for you in My life from start to finish, in every single detail.

Love,

God

DEEPER STUDY

- Read John 14:1-11.

POINT TO PONDER

- In what ways can you see God's love for you through Jesus' life and not just His death?_____

_____

_____

_____

_____

_____

_____

_____

_____

_____

_____

_____

_____

_____

_____

_____

_____

_____

_____

CHAPTER 10

YOUR NEW BEST FRIEND

Now, most people would not be willing to die for an upright person,
though someone might perhaps be willing to die
for a person who is especially good. But God showed his great love
for us by sending Christ to die for us while we were still sinners. And since we
have been made right in God's sight by the blood of Christ, he will certainly
save us from God's condemnation. For since our friendship with God was restored
by the death of his Son while we were still his enemies,
we will certainly be saved through the life of his Son.
So now we can rejoice in our wonderful new relationship
with God because our Lord Jesus Christ has made us friends of God.
—Romans 5:7-11

Dear Loved One,

It is one thing to give away something you love dearly. It is another to watch that very thing be destroyed. I did both because I love you.

I gave My Son, sent Him to be born in the world, and all He ever did was love people and minister and heal, teach, and preach and show people the way to the best of kingdoms. Yet they clawed at Him, the perfect Son of God; yanked Him around; and nailed Him to a disgraceful cross to die.

I let that happen to Him so you could see My love (John 10:18). I allowed that wicked yet beautiful act to happen.

And in that moment, and in those hours on the cross, I took all the ways that you had ever treated Me—spitting in My face, hating Me, rejecting Me, disobeying Me, being filled with evil intentions, treating people the way they never deserve to be treated—I took all of that and I put that on My Son Jesus (Isa. 53:6; 1 John 2:2).

And because I hate all of those things, I had to turn and look the other way from My Son while He carried and died for the sins of all the world—past, present, and future.

I said, "No," to My Son when He asked for a way out (Matt. 26:39), any way out.

I kept from nodding to the armies of angels I could have sent to rescue Him at a moment's notice (Matt. 26:53).

I let Him feel completely abandoned and alone (Matt. 27:46), this One who is one with Me.

It was enough for Me to give up the hardest thing to give up, but then I even allowed that precious One to be murdered brutally in the most inhumane of ways on the cross.

And all of it? All of it was for completely and utterly undeserving people. This selfless, loving act was for the worst of the worst. It was for those who were still My enemies, even you (Col. 1:21). It was for sinners and rebels and God-haters. Because it was not for good people or friends but enemies that I was dying.

And all of that death and destruction and rebellion that Jesus took on Himself, He was able to carry it away, to destroy it and its demands. Your charges are dropped because of the cross. Even the record of your charges is nowhere to be found, forgiven and erased and cancelled (Col. 2:13-14). Jesus took on your sins so He would be the one crushed and weighed down with them and you could be whole and restored and redeemed.

He became what you were so that you could become what He is, and that is a friend of God, a child of God, a dear one of God (2 Cor. 5:21).

I demonstrated how far My love would go by dying for you, My enemy at the time. And in the process, I made you My friend forever.

Love,

God

DEEPER STUDY

- Read Isaiah 53.
- Read Ephesians 2:1-7.

POINT TO PONDER

- What new benefits do you now have since you are God's friend and not His enemy anymore? _____

_____

_____

_____

_____

_____

_____

_____

_____

_____

_____

_____

_____

_____

_____

_____

_____

_____

_____

_____

_____

_____

_____

CHAPTER 11

THE MOST GOD COULD EVER GIVE

So I am not the one living now—it is Christ living in me.
I still live in my body, but I live by faith in the Son of God.
He is the one who loved me and gave himself to save me.
—Galatians 2:20 (ERV)

Dear Loved One,

No one can give more than themselves to prove their love. And this is just what I gave you when Jesus died for you on the cross.

His life was "cut short in midstream" (Isa. 53:8), right down the middle for you.

The most important life that ever came to be on this earth was the life of Jesus, My Son, and yet I did not consider it to be so important that I would not give it up on your behalf.

Jesus lived for only thirty-some years. He still had so much life that He could've lived. Maybe He even could have chosen to live forever; that wouldn't be impossible for Me. Or I certainly could have rescued Him and brought Him back to Me at any moment.

Instead, He chose to die young.

It was no one that took His life from Him. The soldiers, the Pharisees, the rebels couldn't take it. He laid it down Himself. It was His choice, My choice; it was a holy sacrifice for you made once but good for all times (Heb. 10:10).

No one ever had the power to take that life from Him; He gave it up voluntarily. He could lay it down for you and pick it up again, because He had My power and authority to do that.

And why was it? For love. Only love. Death by love.

But in another way, that life was not cut off at all. By giving His life—by giving Himself—Jesus became a spirit again. So that when you put your faith in Him, the life of Christ continues through the Spirit in you. When Christ died, you died with Him (Col. 2:20). And now that He lives again, He lives on in you (Col. 3:3).

You can say with confidence now, "It is no longer I who live, but Christ lives in me" (Gal. 2:20).

Jesus told His disciples that it was "necessary" (Matt. 16:21) for Him to go to Jerusalem and die. How could it be necessary for the most important human of all history to die so early?

It was necessary for My will, necessary for My love.

But it was not only necessary for Him. He said it was also best for His disciples (John 16:7). He cared more about what was best for them and best for you, the ones I wanted to redeem, than best for Him. And if He died, then His spirit could return and live on in you. And that is just what He did for you.

Out of love, He gave Himself for you so that His life could return and live on in you. He ended His own life so that He could return to Me and then send His Spirit to live on in you. He gave Himself for you (John 10:15).

In this was a transfer of His life into your body. The you inside of you—the God-failing, law-breaking, condemnation-bearing you—has died. In its place you will find living in you Jesus—the God-loving, faith-living, grace-receiving new you.

That life He gave is now yours.

This is great love: giving your own life for another to have life. In fact, there is no greater love than this, My dear (John 15:13).

Love,

God

DEEPER STUDY

- Read John 10:1-18.

POINT TO PONDER

- How does viewing your life as a continuation of Christ's life affect your priorities?_____

_____

_____

_____

_____

_____

_____

_____

_____

_____

_____

_____

_____

_____

_____

_____

_____

_____

_____

_____

_____

_____

_____

_____

CHAPTER 12

REAL LOVE ISN'T A TRANSACTION

*This is real love—not that we loved God, but that he loved us
and sent his Son as a sacrifice to take away our sins.*
—*1 John 4:10*

Dear Loved One,

I've loved you as much as possible; there's no way I could ever love you more than I already do. And even if you never, ever, ever love Me back, My love for you is still the truest of loves.

My love exists on its own; it is what it is apart from your response. It doesn't depend on you receiving it, comprehending it, or returning it. Because real love does not demand reciprocity. It loves the full amount even if unreturned forever.

See, real love begins inside Me. And then, I express it by giving. Yes, love is always giving. It gives away what is valuable to oneself for the benefit of another. It is free of charge, free of expectation, free of record-keeping (1 Cor. 13:5).

This is the ingredient of real love, this and nothing more.

So My love would still be real and genuine and complete even if you and everyone else didn't love Me back. Because it was when you were still sinners—hateful, rebellious, and unloving towards Me—that I set My love on you (Eph. 2:4-5), and it remains on you even if you never turn from sinner to saved one.

My love exists and remains independent of who it rests on or the response they give. It does not have to be mutual to be real.

And, in fact, My love will never be returned in the amount that it was given. Love is not even; it doesn't end in ties. You will never be able to love Me equal to how I've loved you. Still, I give you My love freely.

This is a love, though, that everyone who receives with open hands will be changed by. They will love as well. It is a love that, when known, transforms the one loved. Just knowing Me, Love, brings about love in you.

It is a love that never lessens or subtracts; it can only be multiplied. It begins in Me and then goes to you and then, through you, carries on to others.

My love for you is the real thing. Because it loves you even though you don't deserve it and can't earn it; even when you were far away from Me and even when you love Me imperfectly now, My love never fades or shrinks.

That's how I can keep on and keep on and keep on loving you when you make mistakes because none of that matters: I haven't changed. So My real love hasn't changed either.

Because this is real love: to love on the basis of Love itself, not the one you are loving. And because I love you on the basis of My unchanging love, I will always love you with this kind of real love.

Love,

God

DEEPER STUDY

- Read 1 Corinthians 13:4-7.

POINT TO PONDER

- How is "real love" different from what you've always thought love was?

_____

_____

_____

_____

_____

_____

_____

_____

_____

_____

_____

_____

_____

_____

_____

_____

_____

_____

_____

_____

_____

_____

_____

_____

_____

_____

_____

_____

_____

_____

_____

_____

CHAPTER 13

WHY GOOD THINGS HAPPEN TO BAD PEOPLE

The Lord is kind and merciful.
He is patient and full of love.
He does not always criticize.
He does not stay angry with us forever.
We sinned against him,
but he didn't give us the punishment we deserved.
His love for his followers is
as high above us as heaven is above the earth.
And he has taken our sins
as far away from us as the east is from the west."
—Psalm 103:8-12 (ERV)

Dear Loved One,

You are quick to ask Me why I allow evil and bad things and hard situations to happen to you, especially if I love you. But what about when I allow good things to happen to you every day, even though you offend Me every day?

I have given you My laws, commands, and guidelines for you to follow to live life in a right way. I gave My laws and commandments for the world written on your hearts and in My Word.

But before you knew Me and even now, you daily break those laws. You daily offend a holy and good God who desires for you to have righteousness, goodness, and a character like Mine because I know that is good for you. For this reason, you were made, in fact: to be like Me (Gen. 1:26)!

But you are so infinitely unlike Me on your own because you choose to oppose Me and reject Me and to do the evil that you should not do instead of the good that you know you should (James 4:17).

It is a wonderful thing then that every day, any day, you are allowed to live on this green earth I created to be filled with people like Me. I bear with you because I am merciful. It is a sheer act of mercy, a clear demonstration of My patience and slowness to anger and display of My love that I do not every day accuse you or burst out in anger or punish you or deal with you the way you deserve.

I let the sun wake up and rise and shine on both wicked and righteous people (Matt. 5:43-48). I provide food for them. I give them clean water and warm shelter and people to love.

This is My love, a love that chooses still to love those who constantly demonstrate that they do not have love for Me in return. Yet everyone has been a person who, at some point in their lives, constantly rejects the kindness and mercy and love I have for them.

Still, My love for you is a love that—time and time again, even in the face of rejection—chooses still to love you and to pursue you and to give you an opportunity to be Mine. Even in your moments of rejection, I don't desire to be separated from you; I'm willing for you to come to Me and experience My love and salvation because Christ has restored us to each other now.

Instead of the condemnation and curses you deserve, I have given you My righteousness and every blessing through your restoration to Me in Jesus Christ (Eph. 1:3).

From the moment you were born, you were born into sin. You were born as My enemy. But I loved you even then and provided you with good things even then: when you hated Me.

Because My love is perfect. And it allows good things to happen to bad people. I continually show My kindness even to people who hate Me, all in the hopes that My kindness will lead them to a life of turning from their old ways and turning to Me, finally (Rom. 2:4)!

I let good happen to them so that they will see Me, turn to Me, and know Me; that's what I've done for you.

Love,

God

DEEPER STUDY

- Read Romans 2:1-4.

POINT TO PONDER

- Are there any good things God has done for you that you've never thought about before?_____

_____

_____

_____

_____

_____

_____

_____

_____

_____

_____

_____

_____

_____

_____

_____

_____

_____

_____

CHAPTER 14

LOVE WILL CHASE YOU DOWN

*Surely your goodness and unfailing love will pursue me
all the days of my life, and I will live in the house of the Lord forever.*
—Psalm 23:6

Dear Loved One,

Yes, My love has been with you for all of your life, even when you didn't know it. Look behind you, and My love is there even now.

Even when you've wandered for days, for weeks, for months, for years, My love hasn't stopped chasing you down. Even when you didn't know Me, or you hated Me, My love was already coming for you.

My love is not far from anyone. My hand is never too far away to reach for you and for you to reach back and take it (Acts 17:27). I will guide you on the right paths every day in My love. I will hold you in My hands, and nothing will be able to take you out of them.

My love isn't like human love; it doesn't get tired. I am not a God who grows tired and weary and exhausted by running after people, no matter how fast they are running away from Me.

I am the Good Shepherd, and I will go great lengths to find My sheep when they wander away from Me and get lost. I will go to great lengths and great distances for you.

I will search for you until I find you, near and far. I won't lose heart halfway through the journey and then turn back around to go home empty handed. No, I go to search for the one who is lost until I find them (Luke 15:4).

I will walk through the fields and the rivers and the valleys to get to you.

I will not give up along the way. For "love never gives up, never loses faith, is always hopeful, and endures through every circumstance" (1 Cor. 13:7).

I will find you.

And when I find you, I will get you out of the rocky cliff where you are stuck. I will free you from the pit you've fallen into and couldn't get out of, the place the wolves soon would have found you.

I will lift you up over my head, securing you on My strong shoulders. And with joy in My heart, I will carry you back to where you belong: at home with Me. Because I love you.

That is why My love pursues you tirelessly: so you can be with Me.

Love,

God

DEEPER STUDY

- Read Psalm 23.
- Read Luke 15:1-7.

POINT TO PONDER

- What measures of love has God taken to bring you closer to Him?___

_____

_____

_____

_____

_____

_____

_____

_____

_____

CHAPTER 15

WHY YOU HAVE TO BE BROKEN APART (BEFORE YOU CAN BE PUT BACK TOGETHER)

Thank the Lord for his faithful love
and for the amazing things he does for people.
—*Psalm 107:8, 15, 21, and 31 (ERV)*

Dear Loved One,

It is easy to see My love in the healing and the rescuing and the saving. But do you see Me, as well, in the brokenness and struggle and captivity?

Before you ever knew Me, before you were ever aware that I was active in your life, I was active in your life nevertheless.

Whether you were like those wandering in the wilderness—lost and homeless, hungry, and thirsty and aware of your spiritual and total need for Me.

Or whether you were like those who were adamantly rebellious against Me and angry with Me and breaking My law in contempt of Me and miserable because of it.

Or whether you were stuck with the consequences of your sin, at the end of your rope, and ready to give up.

Or maybe you were too busy for Me—off traveling the world and trying to find all that you could in it instead of in Me (Ps 107).

No matter who you were, I came for you. I pursued you. I allowed you to come to the point in your very specific life that you recognized your need for Me.

I let you get stuck in the thicket or fall into a hole or break your leg so that you would be in a situation that only I, the Shepherd, could fix. I let you grow desperately hungry and thirsty for Me (John 6:35).

And this is the great miracle of any life: to finally come to a point of wanting Me and needing Me and calling out to Me, "Lord, help me!" For after the world turned dark with sin, no one on their own can ever do that. None of the people in this world choose to look for Me (Rom. 3:11).

It is the circumstances in your life that I was always moving in and always orchestrating that brought you to a place of recognizing and seeing Me for the first time in your life.

And why did I do this? Because of My great love for you—even when you were against Me or unaware of Me altogether.

You are thankful for My "faithful love" for you and for the "amazing things" I do for you (Ps. 107:8, 15, 21, and 31). But the amazing things are not only the moments of healing and the moments of rescue and the moments of resolution. They are the moments of brokenness and hurt and disappointment that preceded the moments of restoration.

All of your moments of hurt, brokenness, and rebellion, I have not allowed them to push you away from Me, but to push you towards Me so you will see your need for Me, come to Me, and be loved by Me. Even those hard days were messages of My love to you.

It is in front of the background of your dark history that the light of My grace becomes all the more glorious and marvelous in your life; this is how I have loved you.

Love,

God

DEEPER STUDY

- Read Psalm 107.
- Read Romans 3:10-18.

POINT TO PONDER

- What was a hard moment that God let you experience so that you would come to Him?_____

_____

_____

_____

_____

_____

_____

_____

_____

_____

_____

_____

_____

_____

_____

_____

_____

_____

_____

_____

_____

_____

_____

_____

CHAPTER 16

WHEN GOD RUNS, HE RUNS TOWARD YOU

So he returned home to his father.
And while he was still a long way off, his father saw him coming.
Filled with love and compassion, he ran to his son, embraced him, and kissed him."
—Luke 15:17

Dear Loved One,

My love always comes for you. And when you finally turn around and start coming towards Me, I run for you.

The best way I can describe this love that runs for you is with a story, one you may have heard before. It goes like this:

He had probably played it out in his head for the whole walk back, the miles of dusty roads leading to an old, too familiar place.

Okay. I'll walk up the driveway and probably see one of the servants working up in the garden, and they'll go running and tell him that I'm here. So I'll have time to get to the porch and walk up the stairs and he'll probably be standing there, looking at me very disappointed. He's probably going to say, "I tried to tell you not to go" or "I knew this would happen" or "What are you doing here?" I don't really know what he'll say.

Hmm. Then maybe I should talk first. Okay. What should I say? "Hey, Dad. How's it going?" No. "I'm sorry." Umm. "Father, I know I messed up. Big time. I really blew it with you. You have a right to be angry." Maybe I'll see how he responds and if he still looks angry, then I can just tell him, "You know, I know I don't deserve to be your son anymore. I can just be one of the servants. Please, please hire me." I just know he's going to be so disappointed. But he usually needs help this time of year with all the harvest; that's my only real chance.

But what happened, what really happened, he probably never pictured.

He was walking towards the house where he grew up, towards the brothers and sisters and servants he knew, and towards the father that he had despised by taking his inheritance before he was even dead. He was walking slowly, like a dog with his tail between his legs, now at the edge of the drive.

When his eyes finally lifted, he noticed someone was there rocking in his favorite chair on the front porch. It was his father. And he was sitting there as if he had been sitting there every day since he left, waiting and looking to see if by some chance his son would come home today.

He rose from his chair, staring out across the field at his son, searching his face to make himself believe it could really be him. And when their eyes met, and they recognized one another, he stopped in his tracks. The father held the stare. Then he did something his son never would've dreamed in 1,000 years.

He walked to the edge of the porch, descended the stairs in a swift leap, and took off running in his direction. Right for him. He didn't know what to do. He hadn't expected this; was his father angry?

When his father got to him—before he had even a moment to respond or show respect—his father grabbed him up in his arms into the longest, strongest, and tightest hug that he had ever given his son and spun them both around.

The son's eyes filled with tears, as he began to struggle and stumble over his practiced speech. A lump caught in his throat, but he managed to get through the first few words: "Father, I-I-I don't deserve . . . " he started, shaking his head. "I have sinned against you, and I've sinned against heaven—I don't deserve to be called your son anymore. Please—"

But his father wouldn't hear it. He cut him off before he could finish.

He turned to the servants who had been gathering around, and he began exclaiming like a happy, crazy person, "Bring the best robe! Oh, and the ring from the chest! Don't forget his sandals! Get dinner ready. My son has come home!"

And almost as if no time had passed at all, no sins had been committed, and no offense had been made, father and son walked together, arms over shoulders, into their home together to live out all their lives.

That's Me. That's My love for you. That's My welcome embrace when you return to Me where you belong.

I run and grab you up in My arms and forgive you. I come to you faster than you can say, "Lord, I need you." I come faster than you can get out all your apologies and confessions and promises to serve Me. I'm already running to you, My heart filled with love.

When you walk to Me, I run to you, My dear one.

Love,
God

DEEPER STUDY

- Read Luke 15:11-32.

POINT TO PONDER

- What mistakes from your past make you believe God could never love you again? How does this story speak to you?_____

_____

_____

_____

_____

_____

_____

_____

_____

CHAPTER 17

FORGIVEN FOR ALL YOUR SINS

Once we, too, were foolish and disobedient.
We were misled and became slaves to many lusts and pleasures.
Our lives were full of evil and envy, and we hated each other.
But—When our Savior revealed his kindness and love, he saved us,
not because of the righteous things we had done, but because of his mercy.
He washed away our sins, giving us a new birth
and new life through the Holy Spirit.
He generously poured out the Spirit upon us through Jesus Christ our Savior.
Because of his grace he made us right in his sight
and gave us confidence that we will inherit eternal life.
—Titus 3:3-7

Dear Loved One,

I am an exceptional account-keeper. And yet I give you a clean slate when you become Mine and every time you receive My forgiveness, which I give to you because I love you.

You need forgiveness often; you've sinned every day of your life. You were born a sinner. From day one, you have chosen over and over again to offend and disobey Me, the One has given you all you have and loved you for eternity.

Imagine you owed Me only $1 every time you sinned.

Every time you hated someone in your heart.

Every time you lied.

Every time you lusted.

Every time you got angry with someone without a good reason.

Every time you loved something more than you love Me.

Even if you only sinned ten times a day, now you would owe Me tens of thousands or even hundreds of thousands of dollars.

Yet the real expense of your sin is death. Even if you had sinned only once, you would deserve the death penalty because, since the very beginning, death has been set as the price for sin, the cost, the trade-in for choosing sin (Rom. 6:23).

You deserve a million deaths for your countless sins; you could never pay Me back with a thousand lifetimes.

Doing a few good things here and there won't make up for it.

The only way you could ever be in the clear is if you could pay it all back somehow or the debt could be canceled.

I've done them both for you, loved one.

Jesus died all your deaths on the cross, pouring out innocent blood for the crimes you had stacked up on your name. And since the price was paid in full, your account was balanced out and made clear.

His death had to cover all your sins: not just the ones from the past, but the ones you commit today and the ones you will commit tomorrow. Otherwise, even one sin left unnoticed would condemn you to death again.

But there is no condemnation for those who have believed in Jesus and belong to Me (Rom. 8:1).

There is no debt owed (Col. 2:14).

There is no death required.

I, your loving Father, have washed away your sins, and you get an account of righteousness. Christ became your sin so you could become His righteousness (2 Cor. 5:21).

I don't even remember your sins anymore. They're forgiven, forgotten, floating somewhere at the bottom of an ocean of grace never to see the light of day again.

I look at you—once disobedient, evil, and hateful—and I see a new person through the lens of My love, a person who is forgiven and made righteous just as I am righteous.

Love,

God

DEEPER STUDY

- Read Matthew 18:21-35.

POINT TO PONDER

- How does God respond to you now when you receive His forgiveness?

_____

_____

_____

_____

_____

_____

_____

_____

_____

_____

_____

_____

_____

_____

_____

CHAPTER 18

THIS IS NEW, REAL LIFE

But God is rich in mercy, and he loved us very much.
We were spiritually dead because of all we had done against him.
But he gave us new life together with Christ. (You have been saved by God's grace.)
Yes, it is because we are a part of Christ Jesus
that God raised us from death and seated us together with him in the heavenly places.
—Ephesians 2:4-6 (ERV)

Dear Loved One,

My love makes you alive. Really alive.

It seems nonsensical when you think about it: you were already living when you accepted My grace into your life. You had a heartbeat and brain activity and lungs taking in air.

By all outward appearances, you were alive.

But there is another life that cannot be measured by these outward vital signs.

You were dead before. Dead in sin. Hopeless and apart from Me and lost.

Still, you have never yet known what it's like to be outside of My love. Because I have always loved you. Even before you knew Me.

But before you knew Christ Jesus, you were on your way to a place where My love is not protecting you anymore, a place called hell. That is where they go who never accept My love for them nor believe in My Son. They choose to remain in sin; they choose to remain as My enemy.

Ultimately, My love will allow them to make that decision to reject Me: love does not "demand its own way" (1 Cor. 13:5), even when that way is right and good and best.

And you would have been with them there, because you were dead, too. You could only be brought to life when you were born again—renewed and brought to true life in your spirit. And this is the life that I have given you in Jesus Christ. I have saved you from what you were and what you were destined for!

Now, you are really alive.

This is the life that doesn't end.

This is the life that doesn't have only sixty or seventy years under its belt.

This is the life that begins when you are born again by My Spirit, becoming new and alive.

And this new life exists somehow in a place you've never been to. Your spirit was raised when Christ was raised from the dead, and your spirit is already seated with Him in the "heavenly realms" (Eph. 2:6).

Because this life, this eternal life, is in knowing Me. As Jesus Himself said, the only way to have eternal life is by knowing Me, "the only true God," and by knowing Him, "the one [I] sent to earth" (John 17:3).

So you have real and true life now, real and true life that is located with Christ and found in Christ and synonymous with Christ. You are restored and redeemed and brought back to the relationship you were made for. You are united with Christ, and this means you have become part of the fulfillment of My greatest purpose, My greatest plan, from the very beginning: to bring everything to its rightful place in Christ.

Now you are really alive, living the life I always intended for you. Because My love makes you truly alive.

Love,

God

DEEPER STUDY

- Read John 3:1-17.
- Read Colossians 3:1-17.

POINT TO PONDER

- How is "being alive" different now that you know Christ? _____

_____

_____

_____

_____

_____

_____

_____

_____

_____

_____

_____

_____

_____

_____

_____

_____

_____

_____

_____

_____

_____

_____

_____

CHAPTER 19

A CONSTANT REMINDER OF LOVE

For we know how dearly God loves us,
because he has given us the Holy Spirit to fill our hearts with his love.
—Romans 5:5b

Dear Loved One,

You know when you try to tell someone you love them, and you just can't seem to find all the right words?

So maybe you try to find another way.

You write them a love letter.

Or you send them a gift.

Or you kiss them all over the face again and again.

Still, it just won't do.

Well, I have done those things for you to know My love, as well. Yes, I have given you My love letter, sent My most prized Son as a gift to you, and kissed you with blessings to remind you of My love every day.

But I also have a great advantage in sharing My indescribable love with you! Because I can even put My love directly into your heart, right inside of you.

When you believe in Christ and become My child, I make My own home inside of you. My Holy Spirit moves in to live in you, and He fills your heart with love straight from Me. Directly, fully, and freely.

With My Spirit inside of you, you can know how I feel about you, what I think about you, and what I want for you at any time, every moment.

Love. It's all love.

The Holy Spirit doesn't speak words of condemnation to you.

Or words of fear.

Or words of deception.

Those voices aren't Mine.

The Holy Spirit speaks the truth about who I am and who you are now (John 14:15-17): I am your loving Father, you need Me desperately, and I am with you (Rom. 8:15). Always.

And even when other voices compete with My voice inside you, you can know the truth. You can hear the voice of truth. It is there, greater than your feelings if you will listen.

That is one reason I have given you My own Spirit: so you can hear the truth about My feelings for you. And more than that, so you can have strength to receive My love, to believe My love, to grow in My love, to understand My love, and to experience My love (Eph. 3:16-19).

I have put My own Spirit, My own self, inside you so that you can always be reminded of My love for you. It's an always reminder of an always love.

Love,

God

DEEPER STUDY

- Read 1 Corinthians 2:6-16.

POINT TO PONDER

- How does God personally remind you of His love?_____

_____

_____

_____

_____

_____

_____

_____

_____

_____

_____

_____

_____

_____

_____

_____

_____

_____

_____

_____

_____

_____

_____

_____

_____

CHAPTER 20

THE TRUTH ABOUT WHO YOU ARE

"See how very much our Father loves us, for he calls us his children,
and that is what we are! But the people who belong to this world
don't recognize that we are God's children because they don't know him."

—*1 John 3:1*

Dear Loved One,

I know other people can make you feel like you're lesser, unwanted, unimportant. They fail at loving you the way I do: with a constant recognition of who you truly are and how you really ought to be treated.

And even if they never meant to do it, you've picked up on all the messages through what they said to you and how they treated you all these years. And when you're around those messages long enough, you might even begin to believe them, too.

Even the Evil One, My enemy, is known as "The Accuser" (Rev. 12:10), constantly speaking words against you of blame and untruth about who you are.

And those in this broken world can't recognize the family resemblance between you and Me because they don't know Me, your Father. Of course, they can't figure out we're related or who you are!

The truth is that no matter how anyone treats you or what they have said about you, that doesn't change the reality of who you are. Even if you've started to believe the lies, that doesn't change the reality of who you are either.

Because I've already made up My mind about who you are. I have already decided who you are and made you who you are and spoken up about who you are. And you can believe that what I have said about you is 100 percent true.

Even if they say you are unsightly, I say you are "wonderfully" made (Ps. 139:14).

Even if they say you don't matter, I say you are valuable to Me (Matt. 6:26).

More than anything, even if they get it all mixed up and say you are evil just as they said of Jesus (John 10:20), I say you are one of My own children, holy and like Me (1 Pet. 2:9).

And nothing can change these realities about who you are, My dear.

This is My great love for you: not only that I have called you My child, but that I have really made you My child. This is your identity now. As surely as Jesus is My child, now you are My child, as well.

Oh, I hope you can really believe who you are in Me every day, that your view of yourself would not be shaded by the world but lit up by the truth of My love for you.

Only then, through the viewpoint of My love, can you see who you really are.

Love,

God

DEEPER STUDY

- Read John 1:10-13.

POINT TO PONDER

- The Bible has many descriptions for believers: we are God's children, citizens of His kingdom, living stones, His holy people, and more. Which part of your true identity in Christ resonates with you? _____

_____

_____

_____

_____

_____

_____

_____

_____

_____

_____

_____

_____

_____

_____

_____

_____

_____

_____

_____

_____

_____

_____

_____

_____

_____

_____

_____

_____

_____

CHAPTER 21

HOW FEARS FALL AWAY

And as we live in God, our love grows more perfect.
So we will not be afraid on the day of judgment,
but we can face him with confidence
because we live like Jesus here in this world.
Such love has no fear, because perfect love expels all fear.
If we are afraid, it is for fear of punishment,
and this shows that we have not fully experienced his perfect love.
—1 John 4:17-18

Dear Loved One,

You do not need to be afraid anymore, because My love is here taking away every fear.

The only thing I have ever commanded you to fear, in all of history, is Myself—to have a healthy fear of the One who holds the destiny of your soul in His hands (Matt. 10:28). But My perfect love, as it enters your life and consumes who you are, kicks out every fear you have—even your fear of Me, in a sense.

Because you don't have to fear the "day of judgment" (I John 4:17) when you stand before Me to give an account of what you have done with your life, every word you've spoken and every thought you've kept hidden inside. You will stand before Me unafraid, unashamed, unembarrassed.

You will stand before Me with confidence because you are like Jesus, changed by My love to reflect Him like a mirror.

Righteous.

Holy.

Loved.

Now think about the smaller things you fear. Every fear is not fear of what you say you are afraid of, but rather the outcome or reaction you expect to happen as a result.

You're not really afraid of spiders. You're afraid of getting poisoned and sick from their bite.

You're not really afraid of heights. You're afraid of falling.

You're not really afraid of speaking in public. You're afraid of being laughed at if you stumble over your words.

These are smaller fears in your life, but still real to you. Yet if I have taken away your biggest fear, I will take these away, as well.

Since you live in Christ, you have no reason to fear the outcome of standing before Me. I have planned from long ago to present you to Myself "holy and without fault" (Eph. 5:27). This is the ultimate outcome for you, for your life. You will be acquitted, deemed not guilty, and freed forever.

And if this fear is gone—the fear of dying and facing condemnation and separation from Me—then what fear could remain? What fear could come between us (Rom. 8:38)?

You don't need to fear what will happen tomorrow.

You don't need to fear what your children will grow up to become.

You don't need to fear what others will say when you turn the corner.

You are free and fearless because of Me and My love in you.

Love,

God

DEEPER STUDY

- Read Romans 8:15-17, 38-39.

POINT TO PONDER

- How does God's love for you address the fears you're holding onto?____

_____

_____

_____

_____

_____

_____

_____

_____

_____

_____

_____

_____

_____

_____

_____

_____

_____

_____

_____

_____

_____

_____

_____

_____

_____

CHAPTER 22

FREE TO LOVE IN GOD'S SAME FEARLESS WAY

We know how much God loves us, and we have put our trust in his love.
God is love, and all who live in love live in God, and God lives in them . . .
We love each other because he loved us first.

—*1 John 4:16, 19*

Dear Loved One,

There's hardly a greater enemy to love than fear. But as I've said, I cast that out of your life with My own love. And then you are free to love fearlessly, too.

Fear will keep you from loving because when you are afraid, you are focused on how you feel and how you think about the situation. You are afraid of the outcome, too.

The fears that can keep you from love are many. Maybe you are afraid that you will not be loved in return. Maybe you are afraid that the other person will see you for who you are. But more than that, maybe you are afraid that they will see you for who you are and reject you.

That you won't be enough.

That you won't have enough to give.

That your love won't be enough to keep them here.

Love casts out these fears, because love is never motivated by getting loved in return. It is always about the giving, just like My love for you. So love is fear-proof.

And love is not afraid of punishment. It's not afraid of being reprimanded or treated with hurt in response to your failings.

Yes, you are imperfect.

You have made mistakes.

You do not really deserve the love that others can give you and certainly not the love I have given you.

But love has never been about earning it. Love comes from Me, and I have loved you first, though you didn't earn it or deserve it (Rom. 5:8). Now, you can love because of that love—that love that chose you and accepted you not for who you were or what you had done but for its own sake.

I chose to love you, and I wasn't afraid of whether or not you would return My love; I gave it freely, knowing that some would never return it. And it's because of My love that you can learn to live in the same way with a love that is unafraid of who you are and unafraid of what others will see and unafraid of what others will do in response to the love that you give. Because you have already been loved.

Love is not afraid. Love knows that love comes from a place of being secure in who you are because of whose you are, and you belong to Love Himself. Because I have loved you and put that love in you, you can love without fear.

You have already been loved with every measure of love that can be given. Please know this. There's no love I've reserved or hidden away from you. There's no way I could love you more than I already do because I already love you fully.

So if she never loves you back, or if he never loves you back, or if they hurt you and trample your heart, if they reject you after seeing who you are, there may be hurt, there may be pain, there may be a sense of rejection.

But no, no, no: there is never a lack of love.

You have never been unloved.

You are not unloved now.

You will never be unloved.

This is the greatest fear: being unloved. And because My love in you casts out this fear and reminds you that you are loved already, you can begin to love others with the same fearlessness and boldness and audacity as I do.

My love is fearless, and it makes you fearless. Because love casts out every fear, even the fears that otherwise hold you back from loving.

Love,

God

DEEPER STUDY

- Read 1 John 4:7-21.

POINT TO PONDER

- How does being able to love like God change the way you can love others?_____

_____

_____

_____

_____

_____

_____

_____

_____

_____

_____

_____

CHAPTER 23

BECOMING ALL YOU'RE MEANT TO BE

*And may you have the power to understand, as all God's people should,
how wide, how long, how high, and how deep his love is.
May you experience the love of Christ, though it is too great to understand fully.
Then you will be made complete with all the fullness
of life and power that comes from God.*
—Ephesians 3:18-19

Dear Loved One,

You are not full yet, because you have yet to fully experience My love in Christ for you.

You will never be made full and complete by finding the perfect spouse.

Or the perfect job.

Or the perfect house.

Or the perfect car.

Or the perfect fitness plan.

You are finally made full and complete and all you were ever meant to be when you find My love, daily.

You begin to find it to the degree that you understand that you have only begun to find it.

The more You understand My love, the more You understand that You do not understand it yet.

It is an infinite love.

An unfailing love (Ps. 145:8).

An eternal love.

An unending love.

An undying love.

An endless love.

I love you with an amount of love that could never be measured—not in pounds or inches or meters or cups or gallons or even light years. It is too much to be counted or tallied up or organized.

So, if My love is immeasurable, you can only imagine how big My heart must be, and I love you with all My heart.

You can understand that My love is immeasurable even if you can't understand how it works. And as you're caught up in the wonder of it all, you become complete, powerful, filled with the life I've always planned for you.

For My love was always there loving you, even before you existed. It's the most permanent thing about you. When you finally begin to understand this love, all the pieces fall together. The picture makes sense. You uncover My great purpose for your existence: to be loved and to love.

In My love, I desire to restore you, eradicate your emptiness, and fill your life with Myself. I want you to be full of My joy, full of My life, and full of all the other good things that compose Me.

I desire to fill you, to break out in the emptiness and darkness of your life with many good things. I want to fill you with all these good things because this is My fullness. This is Me.

And this is why I want you to experience My love moment by moment and day by day. For I know the truth: that you can never become filled without experiencing My love, that part of Me that reveals all the other parts.

So, yes, I want to fill you with many good things. But it is the experience of My love, in particular, that tops it off. It ensures you're the fullest you that you can ever be.

Without My love, you cannot be in Me fully or be fully you. My love, and only My love, makes you all you're meant to be.

Love,

God

DEEPER STUDY

- Read Psalm 63.

POINT TO PONDER

- What helps you grow in your understanding and experience of God's love, personally?_____

_____

_____

_____

_____

_____

_____

_____

_____

_____

_____

_____

_____

_____

_____

_____

_____

CHAPTER 24

CLOSER, CLOSER, CLOSER

*Husbands, love your wives the same as Christ
loved the church and gave his life for it.
He died to make the church holy.
He used the telling of the Good News to make
the church clean by washing it with water.
Christ died so that he could give the church to himself
like a bride in all her beauty.
He died so that the church could be holy and without fault,
with no evil or sin or any other thing wrong in it.*
—*Ephesians 5:25-27 (ERV)*

Dear Loved One,

The greatest act of love you can ever show someone else is to draw them closer to Me. And that is just what Jesus has done for you: He has loved you with a love that has brought us together.

Jesus loved you as He loved Himself. So He wanted you to experience the same intimate relationship with Me that He has always known (1 Cor. 1:9), since before the beginning of time.

He made this possible when He died for you. Now, He has taken you to be His own wife forever, and it's through this relationship that you can discover what it means to be a loving spouse.

From My viewpoint, marriage is for the purpose of making the other person holy. True love not only wishes for holiness for the one it loves, but it also works to accomplish that holiness in them.

You can see this aspect of love in Jesus. He loved you, so He sacrificed Himself on the cross to make you holy in My sight, more like Me.

This was an act of love for you and an act of love for Himself. To Him, you are a part of Himself. He desired for you to experience the full satisfaction found only in My love the way He had experienced it. So He stripped away the filthy rags of sin (Isa. 64:6) and dressed you in a beautiful wedding gown instead, made of His own righteousness. In this way, He made Himself a worthy bride. See, there is always a benefit of drawing others closer to Me.

In bringing you to Me, Jesus also united you with Himself. You became one with Him. You became like Me in that sense, several but only One.

Now, all the benefits of having a close relationship with Me are yours because of this union of Him with you and you with Me (Eph. 1:3).

Jesus' love for you and commitment to you and marriage to you remains unbroken. He does not, will not, and cannot lie; He speaks only the truth. He keeps His word. Christ has sworn Himself to you and taken you to be His wife, and His vows He will never break.

He is faithful, He is true, He is loyal, and He is the love of your life. He watches over you and delights in you and sings over you as a husband still in the honeymoon phase with his wife. And because He loves you truly, He will continue to bring us closer through your marriage to Him.

I hope you will live in the romantic love of Jesus that draws us together every day.

Love,

God

DEEPER STUDY

- Read Ephesians 5:21-33.

POINT TO PONDER

- Based on this chapter, what is the goal of God's love for you?_____

_____

_____

_____

_____

_____

_____

_____

_____

_____

_____

_____

_____

_____

_____

_____

_____

_____

_____

_____

_____

_____

_____

_____

_____

_____

_____

_____

_____

CHAPTER 25

FAITHFUL, EVEN WHEN YOU'RE NOT

Then the LORD said to me, "Go and love your wife again,
even though she commits adultery with another lover.
This will illustrate that the LORD still loves Israel,
even though the people have turned to other gods and love to worship them."
—Hosea 3:1

Dear Loved One,

When you make mistakes, My love for you still doesn't change even then.

That's because it is not a love that is based on your performance. It is a love based on a promise I have made to you and to Myself, My vows of marriage (Heb. 6:13-20).

I will be your God, and you will be Mine.

Christ has patched us up and brought us back together. He has secured your right relationship with Me and your redemption forever (Heb. 9:12-15)!

Your restored relationship with Me is permanent, because I've made a promise – and shook on it with blood on My hands. The blood of Jesus on the cross is the blood of My promise to you.

I always keep My "promises of unfailing love" (Dan. 9:4). I don't break them, no matter what happens.

I am the husband who keeps forgiving My unfaithful wife. Yes, in fact, I already know now that you will run after other lovers in the future. My love makes allowance for your faults (Col. 3:13) and takes the hit for them, too.

But I know there will be a day when you stand before Me pure, innocent, blameless because of what I have done to restore you to Me (Eph. 5:27). Until then, you are the offender. I am the forgiver. You are unfaithful, but I am always faithful. And I cannot deny this part of Myself (2 Tim. 2:13). I don't suddenly change My nature.

For Me to be an unfaithful Husband, I would have to stop being who I am at the core. Because I am faithfulness itself. My faithfulness is as sure as the skies above your head (Ps. 89:2).

But I can't stop being faithful to you, and I won't. I will continue to be faithful, even though you're My imperfect spouse who returns imperfect love to Me.

My love is not based on what you do, but on who I am. And that's why it doesn't change, even for a moment.

I don't love you because of what you do, but because of who I am. That's how I can keep on and keep on and keep on loving you when you sin and turn away from Me, because that doesn't matter: I haven't changed.

Love,

God

DEEPER STUDY

- Read Hebrews 9.

POINT TO PONDER

- How does God's love respond when we are unfaithful to Him?_____

_____

_____

_____

_____

CHAPTER 26

GOD MEETS YOUR NEEDS

"In the same way, husbands ought to love their wives as they love their own bodies. For a man who loves his wife actually shows love for himself. No one hates his own body but feeds and cares for it, just as Christ cares for the church. And we are members of his body."

—*Ephesians 5:28-30*

Dear Loved One,

I love you, and that is an extension of the love I have for Myself, a love that takes care of you as if you were Me.

For I feed you, I tend to you, I care for you, and I meet your needs as I would My own physical body on earth. I certainly care for you, and I see to it that you are fed just as the birds are fed and clothed just as the wildflowers are clothed (Matt. 6:25-30).

But I meet your deeper needs, your soul's needs, as well.

I give you My body, the real bread, to eat. And you will never be hungry again (John 6:35).

I give you My blood, the real drink, to drink. And you will never be thirsty again.

I set out your clothing each morning for you to put on: "tenderhearted mercy, kindness, humility, gentleness, and patience" (Col. 3:12). Most importantly, I set out love for you to put on (Col. 3:14). These are your shirts and pants and socks to wear, and they are yours through Me.

Everything you need is in Me, and I give it all to you without reservation. I give Myself so your needs can be met. Every part of Myself I give to you so you will be nourished and healthy and strong.

Within My church body, I give each person, even you, a specific gift, a specific role, and a specific work. And in fulfilling that work, you join with Me in caring for My body. You fit together just right. You build up the others. Together, you continue to mature. You grow in every way, becoming like Me.

In this way, you all become "healthy and growing and full of love" (Eph. 4:16), My love.

You are constantly being nurtured by Me to become like Me. And when you become like Me, you fulfill your God-given purpose in life And when you become like Me, you become the full person you're meant to be.

And when you become like Me, you bring great praise to My name.

See, when I love you, I am also loving Myself. As I care for you, you gain the strength to do My work. And when you do the work I've given you to do, that brings glory to Me (John 17:4).

As this happens, I share, once again, in the joy of love. And you share, once again, in the glory you were always made for.

Love,

God

DEEPER STUDY

- Read John 6:22-59.
- Read Ephesians 4:4-16.

POINT TO PONDER

- What is the connection between God's love for you and His love for Himself?

_____

_____

_____

_____

_____

CHAPTER 27

NOTHING CAN EVER, EVER COME BETWEEN YOU

No, in all these things we are more than conquerors through him who loved us.
And I am convinced that nothing can ever separate us from God's love.
Neither death nor life, neither angels nor demons,
neither our fears for today nor our worries about tomorrow—
not even the powers of hell can separate us from God's love.
No power in the sky above or in the earth below—
indeed, nothing in all creation will ever be able to separate us
from the love of God that is revealed in Christ Jesus our Lord.
—Romans 8:38-39

Dear Loved One,

My love for you won't let anything keep us apart.

At one time, one thing stood between you and Me: your sin. Because I can't dwell with sin (Ps. 5:4-5)—no more than light and darkness can dwell in the same place. When one is present, the other is not.

But when Jesus died on the cross for your sins, He took the penalty for your sin. He paid the price. He became the sacrifice that took all your darkness on Himself.

You are light now because You believe in Christ.

You are right now because You believe in Christ (Rom. 3:22).

I make people once estranged from Me My friends by grace and faith.

So now that the ugly barrier of sin that separated you from accessing Me freely has been broken down, destroyed, removed, there is nothing standing between you and Me anymore. And nothing can remove you from My presence.

Because that one thing—like a great, far city wall—that was between you and Me was your sin. But I have sledgehammered it apart, broken it down, and bulldozed it away. When Jesus died on the cross, that wall of sin and division was destroyed (Eph. 2:14-18).

Now, you can walk freely through the open door of faith into a place of grace where I long to be with you.

Who can be against you?

Who can condemn you?

What can separate you from My love for you?

The resounding response is "No one and nothing!"

Not the trouble or calamities you face.

Not persecution from others.

Not hunger or destitution.

No danger or threats of death.

Not death or life.

Not angels or demons.

Not your fears for today or your worries about tomorrow.

Not even the powers of hell itself.

Not anything in all creation—for I have decided to set My love on you, and it cannot be removed, severed, or untangled from you.

You already know that even these—the unfavorable, unwanted circumstances, challenges, and conditions of this present life— are instruments of My love, not separators of My love. Not even the most powerful forces can separate you from My unfailing, immeasurable, inseparable love for you.

My love won't let anything come between us ever again. Not now. Not ever.

Love,

God

DEEPER STUDY

- Read Romans 8:31-39.

POINT TO PONDER

- What is keeping you from a deeper relationship with God, and how can His love change this?_____
  _____
  _____
  _____
  _____
  _____
  _____
  _____
  _____
  _____
  _____
  _____
  _____
  _____
  _____
  _____
  _____

CHAPTER 28

LOVE MAKES YOU LIKE JESUS

And we know that God causes everything to work together
for the good of those who love God and are called according to his purpose for them.
For God knew his people in advance, and he chose them to become like his Son,
so that his Son would be the firstborn among many brothers and sisters.
And having chosen them, he called them to come to him.
And having called them, he gave them right standing with himself.
And having given them right standing, he gave them his glory.
—Romans 8:28-30

Dear Loved One,

No matter what you face, no matter what you walk through, no matter what you struggle with, My love remains on you. It's making you like Jesus.

You may be tempted to think that the hard moments and the difficult struggles and the situations you would never choose for yourself are some sort of indication that I have abandoned you, I have forgotten you, or I have rejected you.

Like Jesus, you may scream out to the skies asking Me, "'My God, my God, why have you left me alone?'" (Matt. 27:46 ERV). Even He felt the pain of being away from Me during the biggest challenge of His life.

But it was because of His love for Me that Jesus obeyed and walked to the cross. He asked Me again and again if it was really necessary (Matt. 26:39), and I told Him it was. It was necessary for My will.

And when you make decisions out of love for Me—the love you can have for Me because I have first loved you—I promise the same outcome for your life: that you will be like Jesus, that everything will work out for good, and that you will share in My glory.

Christ was forsaken because all your sin was on Him; so now you are accepted, and you are loved, and you are chosen. I will never forsake or reject you. For the one thing that could stand between us was your sin, and it has all been nailed to the cross and paid for by the blood of Jesus Christ, My dearest Son (Col. 2:14).

No, My dear one, even the hard situations and the difficult moments and the unwanted troubles—I am using even those to demonstrate My love for you. Because My love for you is the love that will continue to conform you to the image of My Son. I will work every situation together for the good of those who love Me and are called according to My purpose for them, and My greatest purpose ever for My people is for them to be in their right place with Jesus.

This is the master plan behind every action, every situation, every event in the history of creation: when it's just the right time, I will "bring everything together under the authority of Christ—everything in heaven and on earth" (Eph. 1:10).

So those difficult situations are not evidence that I am against You; quite the opposite is true. They are evidence that I am uniting you with the same sufferings of Jesus Christ so you can be formed in My image to look like Me (2 Cor. 4:8-11), which is your purpose.

So even those sharp jabs from My love—they aren't cutting you off from Me or keeping you from knowing My love. They are sharpening you!

I am causing all of your difficulties to work for your good for the purpose of making you like Jesus. Because I love you.

Love,

God

DEEPER STUDY

- Read Matthew 26:36-46.
- Read 2 Corinthians 4.

POINT TO PONDER

- What does it mean that God is working all things out for your good?

_____

_____

_____

_____

_____

_____

_____

_____

_____

_____

_____

_____

_____

_____

_____

_____

_____

_____

_____

_____

_____

_____

_____

CHAPTER 29

WHAT EVERY GOOD FATHER DOES

You are children of God, and he speaks words of comfort to you.
You have forgotten these words:
"My child, don't think the Lord's discipline is worth nothing,
and don't stop trying when he corrects you.
The Lord disciplines everyone he loves;
he punishes everyone he accepts as a child."
—*Hebrews 12:5-6 (ERV)*

Dear Loved One,

I love you, so I discipline you to keep you on the right path. I do this for everyone I really love but especially My own children (Rev. 3:19).

You've had a father who disciplined you the best he knew how. But sometimes he didn't discipline you when he should have. Other times, he punished you too harshly when you didn't deserve it; it was really just his anger that he couldn't control, welling up and spouting out.

I'm not like that. I discipline you rightly every time. And the intention behind that is always My desire to make you holy. My discipline is always righteous and needed and fueled by love.

So it is always good for you, too.

These are meant to be "encouraging words" (Heb. 12:5) for you. It should encourage you to know that I discipline you, because when I discipline you, it shows you that I'm treating you as I treat My children. All loving parents have disciplined their children so they would know wrong from right, and I am the ultimate loving Father.

My discipline is not meant to have the effect of turning you away from Me or making you become disheartened.

I know discipline is never enjoyable in the moment. But the discipline I give will grow in you the good seeds that yield "a peaceful harvest of right living" (Heb. 12:11) if you will let them do their work.

Think of Jesus and the way He looked ahead to the outcome rather than focusing on the pain of punishment. He was never punished for His own wrongdoings: He had none on His record (1 Pet. 2:22), not even one. But He still faced punishment: He endured the punishment for all sins (Isa. 53:4-5), the punishment of death, while still holding on to hope. In this way, He showed you a perfect example.

What was it that encouraged Him during the punishment on the cross? It was the thought of the joy still ahead of Him (Heb. 12:2). Jesus could see what would come by way of the cross—that is, the punishment—and to Him, the reward was far greater than the expense.

He accomplished My will.

He brought many children into My glory (Heb. 2:9-10).

He prepared a seat of honor for Himself next to Me, His Father, for eternity.

When you think of all He suffered, taking on your punishment, you have reason to hope, to carry on, to keep going. Because you can see the reality of it all: I discipline you, but on the other side of that discipline is a harvest of righteousness and a sweeter closeness to Me.

Yes, I discipline you because I love you, and I want you to experience more of Me.

Love,

God

DEEPER STUDY

- Read Hebrews 12:1-13.

POINT TO PONDER

- What is God's intention when He disciplines you as one of His children?

_____

_____

_____

_____

_____

_____

_____

_____

_____

_____

_____

_____

_____

_____

_____

_____

_____

_____

_____

_____

_____

_____

_____

CHAPTER 30

THE LOVE OF A LIFETIME

"So remember that the Lord your God is the only God,
and you can trust him!
He keeps his agreement.
He shows his love and kindness to all people
who love him and obey his commands.
He continues to show his love and kindness
through a thousand generations."
—Deuteronomy 7:9 (ERV)

Dear Loved One,

I never stop giving love to you. Not even for a moment of your life.

When you are heartbroken and hurting, I love you.

When you are shattered, I love you.

When you are jumping for joy, I love you.

As you respond to My love by loving Me, I respond to your love by loving you. It is a virtuous cycle of love upon love.

My heart is full of love, and I never run out of love to give. I have it in spades, extras. That is why I can pour it out over others and lavish it on you so extravagantly (1 John 3:1). Because I'm rich in love, loaded with love, overflowing with love.

And I couldn't be happier than to give it to you with an open hand.

And though I give it time and time again, My supply of love never runs low. I have given it away to every generation, from the days of Adam and Eve on up to you and your friends and neighbors. And I could give it away again for another thousand generations.

Still, I have more love to give. My love endures for all time (1 Cor. 13:7). It is enough love for you. In fact, it is more love than you could ever need in this one lifetime.

For it's a love of countless lifetimes, and still it goes on.

Love,

God

DEEPER STUDY

- Read Exodus 34:5-7.

POINT TO PONDER

- What are the limits of the love you can give another person, and what are God's?_____

_____

_____

_____

_____

_____

_____

_____

_____

_____

_____

_____

_____

_____

CHAPTER 31

GOD'S LOVE STAYS—FOR GOOD

But our ancestors became proud and stubborn.
They refused to obey your commands.
They refused to listen.
They forgot the amazing things you did with them.
They became stubborn.
They decided to return to Egypt and become slaves again.
But you are a forgiving God!
You are kind and full of mercy.
You are patient and full of love.
So you didn't leave them!
—Nehemiah 9:16-17 (ERV)

Dear Loved One,

Because I love you, I will never leave you alone.

There will never come a day when I will give up and decide to walk away.

When you are forging through the lowest valley or you are mounting up the highest peak, I am with you. Even when you walk along the darkest path, I am with you (Ps. 23:4). I do not abandon you or leave you on your own.

There are no abandoned children in My family.

Even if your parents have abandoned you or every one of your friends has gone, I am with you and beside you and near to you. And the more you draw near to Me, the more I draw near to you (James 4:8).

Even when the people of Israel were walking their circles around the desert, complaining that I had forgotten, I had not. I was with them even then (1 Cor. 10:1-4). Even when they forsook Me, I did not forsake them. Even when they began to bow down to false gods and give them the credit for all My work and miracles, I did not leave them. My cloud was still there by day and My pillar of fire was still there by night with them, near them, among them.

And so I am with you always—even in your wandering. I don't mind taking the long way with you because I know where the journey ends, and it's always closer to Me. I walk with you and beside you even in your wanderings, even when you get lost, even when you don't know the path.

I say to your heart, "I will never fail you. I will never abandon you" (Heb. 13:5). And that is exactly what I mean.

When you begin to think I have left you, is it because I have? Or is it because the circumstances have changed?

The Israelites complained because they had to leave the place where they were comfortable and then they didn't have the rich, delicious foods they were used to anymore (Exod. 16:3). What they forgot was that when they had the rich foods, they were slaves. And nothing is really better as a slave.

Dry bread for a free man is still better than a buffet for a slave.

I am with you, and I provide for you, even if it's not what you want. And it's enough. Because I am with you and you have no good thing apart from Me (Ps. 16:2), but you have every good thing in Me (James 1:17; 1 Cor. 3:21-23).

Apart from Me, you have no good thing. But you don't have to know what that's like because you will never be apart from Me now. I am with you, and so is My constant presence; it's just one more proof of My love for you.

I will never go, I will never abandon you, and I will never leave. Because I love you, truly.

Love,

God

DEEPER STUDY

- Read Exodus 13:17-22.

POINT TO PONDER

- Why does God's love always choose to stay with us?_____

_____

_____

_____

_____

_____

_____

_____

_____

_____

_____

_____

_____

_____

_____

_____

_____

_____

_____

_____

_____

_____

_____

_____

_____

_____

CHAPTER 32

LOVE IS A VERB

"The love of Christ controls us,
because we know that one person died for everyone.
So all have died. He died for all so that those
who live would not continue to live for themselves.
He died for them and was raised from death
so that they would live for him."
—*2 Corinthians 5:14-15 (ERV)*

Dear Loved One,

My love is a love that compels, that moves.

It stirs and prompts the spirit and heart. My love begins outside of you with Me and then it enters into you through My Spirit (Rom. 5:5). But it is a love that cannot stand still, cannot stay within. It is a love that moves; it is a love with arms and legs.

The church, My dear people, is the body of Christ. It is made up of the parts of Me that go and move and act on My behalf. If the church is the body of Christ, then love is what causes it to move.

Love always urges to action (1 John 3:18); it activates inside but then explodes outside. It needs to be expressed, to continue on, to be shared, to be shown. Love cannot stay quiet and cannot stand still and cannot be unmoved.

My love is a love that compels, that moves.

What should you think about the heart that is untouched by it? You must imagine that the heart that remains still when touched by My love has not truly been touched by that love (1 John 3:17).

If you know Me, you will love (1 John 4:7). If you know My love, you will love. There is no way around it.

My love is not an outward force pushing you. My love holds you together, in one sense, but also it presses you on every side, coming from every direction. On every side, you are pressed in by the love I have for you. And that is how you are held together.

My love surrounds you, moves in you. Then, you move because it is in you.

You can't help but love because My love in you is a love that compels. Yes, it is a love that moves.

Love,

God

DEEPER STUDY

- Read Ephesians 4:11-16.

POINT TO PONDER

- How is God's love moving you?_____

_____

_____

_____

_____

_____

_____

_____

_____

_____

CHAPTER 33

GOD GOES TO WAR FOR YOU

You are my strength; I wait for you to rescue me,
for you, O God, are my fortress.
In his unfailing love, my God will stand with me.
He will let me look down in triumph on all my enemies.
—Psalm 59:9-10

Dear Loved One,

When you go to battle, I go to battle.

When you stand at the front of the battle line, I am standing there with you, beside you. And when you look from face to face at the soldiers beside you, I am in every one of them.

The battle always belongs to Me (2 Chron. 20:15).

As you charge toward the enemy's battalions, I am the strength in you to run.

I am the strength in you to yell out.

I am the strength in you to pull back your bow and send your arrows to the mark.

When the enemy fires back, I protect you. My love is the shield in front of you (Ps. 5:11-12). It protects you. Nothing can break through My love or get past My love. It surrounds you on every side.

When you become tired as the battle rages on, and your soul needs a rest, I am your refuge (Ps. 59:17). I am the place you can run to and lie down and rest and regain your strength (Matt. 11:28).

I am your new mercy in the morning to face the battle again (Lam. 3:22-23).

I am your strength when all your strength is gone (Phil. 4:13).

I am your King who leads you out.

And I am your victory (Rom. 8:37). When you overcome the difficult situation, the "fiery arrows" (Eph. 6:16) from hell, the struggle with sin, it's because of Me: My love in you and My strength in you and My favor towards you is winning for you.

We go to battle together, and My love will always win.

Love,

God

DEEPER STUDY

- Read 1 Corinthians 15:35-58.

POINT TO PONDER

- What are the weapons God uses to fight for you?_____

_____

_____

_____

_____

_____

_____

_____

_____

_____

_____

_____

CHAPTER 34

LOVE LEADS YOU IN GOD'S GOOD PLAN FOR YOU

With your unfailing love you lead the people you have redeemed.
In your might, you guide them to your sacred home.
—*Exodus 15:13*

Dear Loved One,

Every step you take, My love is leading you.

My love knows the way, the course, and the path that's been set out for you. For it has always taken an active role in the planning of it.

I loved you before I made the world, and My love for you has informed every decision I've made since then. To create you, to choose you, to know you, to bring you to this exact moment of your life. And I will continue to lead you because I love you.

Because I love you, I have made a plan for your life from beginning to end (Ps. 139:16). Although, really, I knew you before the beginning, and you'll be with Me even past the end. Our life together will be eternal.

My plan for you, My plan for the world, is Myself (2 Cor. 5:20). I work all things according to the purpose of My plan, and here is the purpose: to bring everything together in Jesus Christ (Eph. 1:10). My plan is to unite everything to Me. My plan is to restore all things to the good relationship they were created for with Me.

I love you, and so I lead you, and My path will always lead you to Me. More of Me.

My desire is that you would know Me more, understand Me more, and look like Me more and more.

I love you, and, as you love Me back, there's a promise in it: a promise that I will work all things together for good in your life (Rom. 8:28). But the promise doesn't end there. The promise to you is that everything in your life will be part of My process to shape you to be like Jesus Christ, My very own beloved and dear Son (Rom. 8:29).

The darkest of nights and the brightest of mornings.

The flooding rains and the beams of sunshine.

The falling tears and the sweet, warm embraces.

I lead you through them all. I work all of them out so that by the end of your life, you'll be more like Christ. And when you see Me, you will be holy and blameless and without fault. And your life will finally come to the end of the path that it was always moving towards: towards Me.

I love you, and, through My love, I lead your life so that you will end up at My doorstep.

Love,

God

DEEPER STUDY

- Read Ephesians 1:3-14.

POINT TO PONDER

- How is God working in your present circumstances to lead you closer to Him?_____

_____

_____

_____

_____

CHAPTER 35

COMPLETE LOVE BECOMES COMPLETE IN YOU

That is how much God loved us, dear friends! So we also must love each other.
No one has ever seen God. But if we love each other, God lives in us.
If we love each other, God's love has reached its goal—it is made perfect in us.
—1 John 4:11-12 (ERV)

Dear Loved One,

Even with all the greatness of My love, it is incomplete right now.

It's not incomplete in the sense that it is lacking in any way. My love is full, and I am full of love (Ps. 86:5). And I am always satisfied with My love. It is an unfailing love. A total love. A romantic love.

But it is a love that's never done, never ended.

My love isn't content with how far it's come; it doesn't end when you receive it. It only finds one more carrier to continue taking it to the others I long to know My love, too.

You are My ambassador (2 Cor. 5:19-20). You have My very thoughts and Spirit and love inside of you, so that you can show them and speak them and share them with others.

This is how you reconcile others to Me.

Because I show love to you, then you are able to love someone else. That is the moment My love has become all it was meant to be from the outset. It was always, always meant to be shared by Me with you and then shared by you with others.

You become an essential part of My love, you carry it on to its rightful conclusion, as you express My love that you have with those in your life.

When you love others, it doesn't make Me love you more. But as you love, you become the completion of My love. And as you become love, you become Me. And we become closer together because we're finally sharing in the joy of My unconditional love.

Yes, even though My love is full, it becomes fulfilled in you.

Love,

God

DEEPER STUDY

- Read John 15:9-17.

POINT TO PONDER

- What part does God desire for you to play in His love?_____

_____

_____

_____

_____

_____

_____

_____

_____

_____

_____

_____

CHAPTER 36

LOVE THAT DOESN'T RUN OUT

But you are a God of forgiveness, gracious and merciful,
slow to become angry, and rich in unfailing love.
—*Nehemiah 9:17c*

Dear Loved One,

Even with all the love I have always given, I always have more love to give you; I've stored away riches of love for you.

You have not reached the end of this road, the bottom of this well, the height of this sky. For even as high as the sky is (Ps. 108:4) and as deep as the oceans are and as far as the east is from the west, even these are less than My love. They fail at showing you the measure of My love for you.

My love is always farther, it's always longer, it's always wider, it's always deeper (Eph. 3:18-19). You have yet to find the bottom or the end or the conclusion of it all.

I am abounding in faithful love. It is part of who I am. So, for as long as I will be, that is how long My love will last and go on in abundance. Though I may give it and give it and give it, I still have more love to give to you. My love does not run out or get used up.

Yes, I revealed My love through Jesus Christ. But you have yet to uncover all of the love even in that strong picture of it. You will search for it and find it and keep finding it in every page of the story.

You will be a student of My love for your whole life and still never know the subject fully as it should be known. Because I am abounding in faithful love. I have more to give, more to show, more to demonstrate, and more to uncover.

Yes, the ocean is deep. But My love is deeper.

Yes, the heavens are high. But My love is higher.

Yes, east is far from west. But My love is farther.

I am unbelievably rich in love with enough to spare for every person for all of time. And still, I have great riches of it.

That is why I will always have more love to give.

Love,

God

DEEPER STUDY

- Read Psalm 36.

POINT TO PONDER

- God's love has been compared to the height of the heavens above the earth. What would you compare His love for you to? _____

_____

_____

_____

_____

_____

_____

_____

_____

_____

CHAPTER 37

EVERY BLESSING IS HERE

Praise be to the God and Father of our Lord Jesus Christ.
In Christ, God has given us every spiritual blessing in heaven.
—*Ephesians 1:3 (ERV)*

Dear Loved One,

Because of My love, I have given Jesus to you. Because I have given Jesus to you, you now have every possible blessing and gift from Me.

I've already given up the hardest thing to give up for you because My love knows no limits. It was willing to give My Son, so it is willing to give anything that I know will be good for you (Rom. 8:31-34).

I dare you to ask Me. Ask Me for anything in My name—anything that would make sense for Me to want for you in light of who I've shown you I am—and I will do it (John 14:14). I will do it.

I will give it with an open hand (Matt. 7:11). My hands are never closed towards you.

I know the needs before you ask (Matt. 6:8). I have the resources before you have the need.

In Jesus Christ, you have become the heir of everything! Here is how it goes: Christ belongs to Me, you belong to Christ, and everything belongs to you (1 Cor. 3:21-23).

Anything you might for a minute think is good, and yet I'm not giving to you, it's not true. I always give you what is best for you, and I know that better than you do, My dear.

Even the good things you have to wait for, I'll give them all to you.

Every good thing you have right now, I have given it to you (James 1:17; Ps. 16:2).

Everything you need to live a godly life for Me, I have given it to you (2 Pet. 1:3).

Every spiritual blessing you could wish for, I have given it to you (Eph. 1:3).

Because of My love, My hands are always open to you. Even now, Jesus stands before Me, pleading for you and praying for you and interceding for you so that I will give you, right now, what you need in Me (Rom. 8:34). And I will.

My love will give you everything you need.

Love,

God

DEEPER STUDY

- Read Psalm 145.

POINT TO PONDER

- What have you believed God is keeping away from you?_____

_____

_____

_____

_____

_____

_____

_____

_____

_____

_____

CHAPTER 38

GOD'S LOVE CARRIES ON IN YOUR FAMILY

You must not bow down to them or worship them,
for I, the Lord your God, am a jealous God
who will not tolerate your affection for any other gods.
I lay the sins of the parents upon their children; the entire family is affected—
even children in the third and fourth generations of those who reject me.
But I lavish unfailing love for a thousand generations
on those who love me and obey my commands.

—Exodus 20:5-6

Dear Loved One,

Just as My love for you began eras ago before you were even born, so My love for you will continue for generations and generations and thousands of years after you have gone on.

See, My love is faithful. But My love is not faithful in the way that you commit your vows: "'til death do us part." Death cannot part you from My love. And it cannot part My love from your family and the generations that will be influenced by the love that I had for you and you returned to Me while you were here.

My love continues and continues and continues.

This is what I mean when I say that My love for you is unfailing, everlasting, and faithful.

My love is such that I will love you no less when you are here living or with Me finally. I will continue to love you and continue to show and demonstrate and share that love with those you leave behind—even those who didn't know you. I will look after your family, see to it that they are loved as you were loved.

Didn't I love Abraham? And didn't I love Isaac? And Jacob? And it was to their descendants that I decided to show love (Mal. 1:1-3), even when they rejected Me time after time.

Creating idols out of jewelry. Testing Me. Forgetting to obey My commandments.

And it was through their descendants that I decided to send the Savior and to keep a people, even when they fiercely rejected Me. I did not stop loving them on behalf of their ancestors.

Remember that. I chose to have their descendants call Me "the God of Abraham, the God of Isaac, and the God of Jacob" (Exod. 3:6) so they would not forget the love I'd had for them even before they were born. They could recognize My love and My continued relationship with them had some part to do with the relationship I had with their ancestors, their family who had lived for generations before them.

I remain faithful to your family and faithful to My love for you, even when you have passed on from this earth to My Kingdom. I give the ones following in your footsteps opportunities to have a relationship with Me. I never forget you.

My love in your life and your returned love for Me leave a legacy that can't be ended.

I will be faithful to continue "the good work" (Phil. 1:6) I began in you until the day of Christ's return for His people, until the whole story of history has been told and a new eternal story has begun.

And when you walk on streets of gold (Rev. 21:21) hand-in-hand with Me, it may be that you will meet those many generations, thousands and hundreds of thousands of people and all their children with them, who were influenced and blessed and benefited by the love I had for you.

For My love for you goes on and on.

Love,

God

DEEPER STUDY

- Read Deuteronomy 7.

POINT TO PONDER

- What do you most hope your children and grandchildren will know about God's love for them?_____

_____

_____

_____

_____

_____

_____

_____

_____

_____

_____

_____

_____

_____

_____

_____

_____

_____

_____

_____

_____

_____

_____

CHAPTER 39

LOVE LASTS FOREVER

Our days on earth are like grass; like wildflowers, we bloom and die.
The wind blows, and we are gone—as though we had never been here.
But the love of the Lord remains forever with those who fear him.
—Psalm 103:15-17a

Dear Loved One,

Yes, My love for you will continue with your family to come once you are gone from this earth, but it will still rest on you, too.

My love will never stop loving you.

Just as you want to be with the ones you love, I want to be with you. I have created a place for that to happen, My own home and city and dwelling place where I wait for you (Heb. 11:16).

After your life here is over, you will come to be with Me there. And in heaven with Me, you'll drink daily from My fountain of love and find it never goes dry.

My love is not a love that wears out, gives up, grows old. My love for you never ends, never stops, never moves on. It "endures forever" (1 Chron. 16:34).

If it is a candle, its flame is always burning.

If it is an ocean, its waves are always turning towards the shore.

If it is the sunrise, its rays are always rising higher.

Just as it has always been there for you, even from eternity ago, so My love will continue to be there, resting on you, in the eternity to come.

There, you will spend every day with Me. We'll finally be together, sharing the love you were always made to experience. You'll feel it like you've never felt it before.

My love for you will always go on. It's as faithful as I am. Forever.

Love,

God

DEEPER STUDY

• Read John 14:1-7.

POINT TO PONDER

• How will your experience of God's love change when you are with Him in His kingdom?_____

_____

_____

_____

_____

_____

_____

_____

_____

_____

_____

_____

_____

_____

_____

CHAPTER 40

HAPPILY EVER AFTER

At that time Jerusalem will be told,
"Be strong, don't be afraid!
The Lord your God is with you.
He is like a powerful soldier.
He will save you.
He will show how much he loves you
and how happy he is with you.
He will laugh and be happy about you,
like people at a party."
—*Zephaniah 3:16-18a (ERV)*

Dear Loved One,

I know there are days, there are moments, when you wish more than anything that you could just see My face, hold My hand, know Me in person. That desire is from Me. And the day for that desire to be satisfied will come soon.

Then, you will never have to know the feeling of what it means to be with Me in spirit but away from Me in presence again. You will come home to Me—in body, mind, and spirit—where your life is already waiting (Col. 3:3), to be in the heavenly places with Me.

I love you, so after this life of experiencing My love on earth, I will bring you to Myself to know My love even closer.

It will be the best wedding day of all time, the moment I've looked forward to for ages. You, My beautiful bride, will come to be with

Me for good. You'll be dressed in white, clothed in Beauty itself, joined to your one True Love.

We'll be married. And you will know My love heart to heart, spirit to spirit, face to face (Rev. 22:4).

I am creating a new place made just for you where we can live our happily ever after together. In My kingdom, we will always be close (John 14:3). You will be able to love Me and praise Me and truly know Me forever.

In heaven, you'll know Me. That is what eternal life is.

See, Jesus came to die to show you I love you. But beneath that, there was a cause: I showed you truly how much I love you by sending My Son so that you could have eternal life in Me (1 John 4:9)! I've given eternal life to those I love and who love Me. But it doesn't just mean your life will never end, that it will go on from now on. But this is about the substance of that life I give you.

Jesus told you the way to have eternal life, the secret for it: it's in knowing Me, the only true God, and in knowing Jesus Christ, the One I sent for you (John 17:3).

Eternal life is in knowing Me personally and in knowing and experiencing My deep love for you. And it is a love you'll continue to learn about every day and then continue to know on a more personal, up-close level once you're finally right here with Me, in the same room.

And I will be so happy with you. I love you because it brings Me joy. And when we're finally together forever, that will bring Me joy, too.

Don't you know that heaven shakes under the dancing feet of the angels when even one person comes to know Me (Luke 15:7)? Just try to imagine the great celebration we'll have together when My whole family comes home to live with Me once and for all.

I'll be dancing, singing, and shouting for joy over you! Because, finally, we'll be in My love the way we were always meant to be in it.

Oh, the best part of our eternity together won't be the streets of gold or the priceless mansions I've built for you or the freedom from crying and fearing and dying (Rev. 21:4); it will be our love, rejoicing that we're finally together, never to be apart again.

Yes, one day soon, our love will find its happy ending; although, in some ways, it will be more like a happy beginning. You will begin to experience in a new way a love that is "better than life itself" (Ps. 63:3), better than all the best days of your life on earth put together.

For you have always been loved—since ages ago, My love. And you are loved right now. And you will be loved for eras to come. Forever and forever, without any slowing down or growing old or giving up, I will love you over and over again.

Love,

God

DEEPER STUDY

- Read Revelations 21:1-22:6.

POINT TO PONDER

- What's been the most impactful aspect you've learned so far about God's love for you?_____

_____

_____

_____

_____

_____

_____

_____

_____

_____

For more information about
Celeste Hawkins
and
Always Been Loved
please visit:

www.ohsunnyceleste.com

Ambassador International's mission is to magnify the Lord Jesus Christ and promote His Gospel through the written word.

We believe through the publication of Christian literature, Jesus Christ and His Word will be exalted, believers will be strengthened in their walk with Him, and the lost will be directed to Jesus Christ as the only way of salvation.

For more information about
AMBASSADOR INTERNATIONAL
please visit:

www.ambassador-international.com
@AmbassadorIntl
www.facebook.com/AmbassadorIntl

Thank you for reading this book. Please consider leaving us a review on your social media, favorite retailer's website,

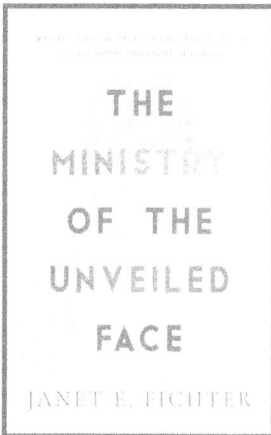

The Ministry of the Unveiled Face grounds us in the simplicity of sharing Christ in the everyday. The meekness of the call lies in our being responsive and obedient to God's prompting as we interact with others. Anchored in persevering prayer, we speak scriptural truths into the lives of others as the Holy Spirit leads. Like the unveiling of a beautiful bride at her wedding, the spiritual veil is removed and Christ's truth and goodness are revealed.

As we walk through dark times in our lives, we all need a way of *Finding Truth in the Tempest.* Faythelma Bechtel knows the tempest, but she also knows the One Who calms the storm. After losing two daughters and her husband, Faythelma has clung tighter to her Savior and longs to help others who are struggling to find peace in their own storms. This devotional journal is not meant to be read as a daily plan, but instead offers meditations on Scripture to help for your unique circumstance.

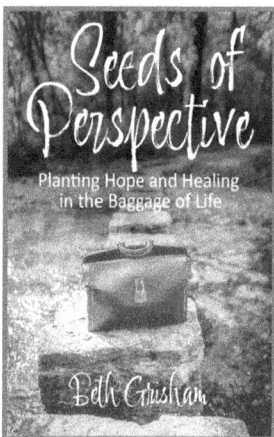

In *Seeds of Perspective,* women of all ages and walks of life willingly poured out their most difficult life situations as a personal sacrifice to help others process and find hope and healing in their own worst mistakes. They believe that remembering and sharing their stories awakens in each of us a deeper understanding of God's promise to redeem our lives for His glory and His purposes and to bring beauty from the ashes of our past.

www.ingramcontent.com/pod-product-compliance
Lightning Source LLC
Chambersburg PA
CBHW072012040426
42447CB00009B/1593